REIMAGINE TECH-INCLUSIVE EDUCATION

EVIDENCE, PRACTICES, AND ROAD MAP

JUNE 2023

ASIAN DEVELOPMENT BANK

ADB

Notes:
In this publication, "$" refers to United States dollars.
ADB recognizes "China" as the People's Republic of China and "Hong Kong" as Hong Kong, China.

Cover design by Jan Carlo dela Cruz. On the cover: Technologies such as Artificial Intelligence (AI) and immersive learning are changing the future of education, accelerated transformation will happen through systemic adoption. (All photos are from ADB unless otherwise stated.)

Contents

Appendixes

Tables and Figures

Foreword

As we tread into the era where digital learning is no longer a choice but a necessity, it becomes increasingly vital to reflect upon the trajectory of technology's role in education, or EdTech, its potential for future progress, and the strategic way we ought to integrate it into various stages of development in our global educational systems.

The COVID-19 pandemic has served as a catalyst, necessitating an expedited evolution in the adoption of digital learning methods. These exceptional circumstances brought about by the pandemic have highlighted the disparities in access, quality, and integration of EdTech across education systems, necessitating an urgent and careful reevaluation of our approach.

The first realization we must acknowledge is the diverse landscape of educational systems worldwide—with each system at different stages of development. It is essential to design interventions that cater to each country's unique requirements and challenges. The approach towards developing a technology-inclusive education system should be both systematic and staged, focusing on a holistic EdTech strategy to create an environment conducive for its effective adoption and usage.

For initial and emerging stages, interventions must focus on creating robust foundational structures, from developing adequate infrastructure to establishing the legal and policy frameworks that guide EdTech implementation. At the same time, efforts must be dedicated to build teacher competencies and community support structures. In contrast, for developed and mature stages, the interventions can be more nuanced, focusing on integrating cutting-edge tools and personalized, adaptive learning methods to facilitate a learner-centered education system.

Looking back, interventions in the education sector, particularly in developing countries, have often suffered from a lack of context and alignment with system needs. It is time to rectify this.

To effectively implement this vision, we must stress two fundamental principles: staged and systematic development and sustainable scaling. Staged development urges caution against a hasty adoption of advanced tools; it promotes a gradual, step-by-step adoption and improvement of digital solutions. It is essential that our approach in developing technology-inclusive education systems is underpinned by strategic decision-making, strong leadership, and comprehensive preparation at all levels.

We need to ensure that interventions are not overly focused on one aspect, such as devices and connectivity, while neglecting others. Systematic development emphasizes a holistic approach, addressing all factors influencing EdTech use concurrently, thereby ensuring cohesive progress and development. The Digital Education Readiness Framework by ADB is recommended as a guiding tool for assessing a country's systematic readiness for digital education and can guide the formulation and implementation of strategies in a well-rounded manner.

Sustainable scaling requires careful selection of EdTech solutions that are affordable, compatible, and aligned with the resource and funding capabilities of the education systems. The Quality, Effectiveness, Scalability, Affordability (QESA) EdTech Evaluation Framework is designed to achieve a methodical, fair, and transparent evaluation and selection process for EdTech solutions that can be scaled nationally.

As we face the challenges and seize the opportunities of this digital era, let this be our guiding philosophy: to reimagine, to evolve, and to excel.

Sungsup Ra
Chief Sector Officer, Sector Advisory Service Cluster
Sustainable Development and Climate Change Department
Asian Development Bank

Preface

The Asian Development Bank (ADB) study "Reimagine Tech Inclusive Education: Evidence, Practices, and Road Map" addresses a crucial topic of great relevance to digital education. At the heart of this study is the quest to better understand what the evidence for effective digital learning is, what are the key interventions and innovations with education technology, and how best to implement effective digital transformation initiatives in the education sector. The study provides a few key ADB frameworks to guide through the digital transformation process including the "Quality, Effectiveness, Scalability, and Affordability" tool kit in identifying and selecting EdTech interventions, the Digital Education Readiness Framework to holistically assess a country's digital education readiness situation, and the Systemic, Staged, and Sustainable strategy recommendations on how to improve the digital capacity through a systemic, staged, and sustainable planning and implementation road map process. The ecosystem approach in digital transformation presented in the paper is the key modality to empower transformative changes in the education sector like what we have witnessed in the electric vehicle sector in recent years.

We bring this piece of research to inform policymakers and practitioners on the important evidence and data driven methodology and the practical corresponding toolkits to capitalize the transformative power of digital learning and teaching. The study drew on various sources of secondary and primary data. It included surveys and literature reviews to integrate evidence, practices and tools through a systematic transformation process framework.

The study used the Digital Education Readiness Framework published in a separate paper "Towards Mature Digital Education Ecosystem" as a foundational benchmarking tool in help assess nationally the country digital situation and gaps across the education ecosystem, and this paper focused on how to systematically improve the digital gaps toward more mature stages of digital education. The findings and recommendations from the study underscore the need for holistically ramp up digital infrastructure, digital content development, teacher digital competency, digital providers and the corresponding enabling digital policy and support from the ministries, to maximize investment output, and avoiding siloed investments or interventions not contextualized to the development readiness stage of the developing countries.

As the leader of this study, I thank the consultant team led by Olli Vallo, CEO and founder of Education Alliance Finland with extensive experiences in EdTech and a wealth of insights for an excellent partnership in this study, together with Stella Lee, Qobil Yunusov, and John Yeo as team members. I also would like to thank Marito Garcia, fellow at the Darden School of Business at the University of Virginia for drafting the initial background paper in 2019.

Brajesh Panth provided valuable guidance to the study. We thank Zhigang Li of the South Asia Department and Vishal Potluri of the Southeast Asia Department as the peer reviewers who provided constructive feedback and suggestions. Dorothy Geronimo coordinated the editorial and publication process.

The study benefited greatly from enriching discussions with government representatives in the respective countries. The findings of the study were shared in country level workshops and Professional Development Planning capacity building workshops with senior officials and key counterparts from developing member countries.

We look forward to discussions in taking forward the study's policy recommendations.

Jian (Jeffrey) Xu
Senior Education Specialist
Sustainable Development and Climate Change Department
Asian Development Bank

Abbreviations

ADB	Asian Development Bank
COVID-19	coronavirus disease
DERF	Digital Education Readiness Framework
EdTech	education technology
EMIS	education management information system
ERP	enterprise resource planning
ESSA	Every Student Succeeds Act
ICT	information and communication technology
LMS	learning management system
QESA	quality, effectiveness, scalability, affordability
SAMR	substitution, augmentation, modification, and redefinition
SDG	Sustainable Development Goal
TPACK	technological, pedagogical, and content knowledge
TPD	teacher professional development

Executive Summary

The rapid pace of digitalization, combined with the spread of the coronavirus disease (COVID-19), has changed digital learning from a choice to a necessity. Education ministries face challenges in measuring progress and understanding how best to benefit from the use of education technology (EdTech) in a way that is fully integrated and aligned with pedagogical practices, governance, and the involvement of all stakeholders.

Today, education systems must address not only the ongoing learning crisis characterized by uneven access and quality challenges but also the recent learning losses caused by the COVID-19 pandemic. In addition, rapid technological advances are causing disruption in the workplace, with tens of millions of jobs involving repetitive tasks or those that can be easily codified at a higher risk of being automated. Therefore, education systems need to adapt to teach the skills necessary for work and good citizenship in society.

The scale of the problem requires more significant changes through more effective ways, as the current methods are insufficient to address the issue of hundreds of millions of students not acquiring basic skills. It is true that some past studies on the role of technology in transforming education have shown mixed results. However, more recent research has generated more positive outcomes from specific generations of technology applications in teaching and learning in the past 20 or so years. Specifically, the most positive impact on learning outcomes has been seen with the third generation of EdTech (from 2014 to 2018), which focused on personalized, adaptive, and blended learning approaches, suggesting that the benefits of technology for education are increasingly evolving. The integration of third-generation technologies such as artificial intelligence and augmented reality/virtual reality in education can be expected to transform traditional teacher-centric models into digital age, learner-centered approaches, with teachers becoming facilitators, coaches, and mentors who empower personalized adaptive learning, improve student engagement, offer individualized feedback, and ultimately prioritize student needs while promoting lifelong learning and increasing global access to educational opportunities.

In fact, the review of 20 meta-analyses of EdTech effectiveness from K–12 to higher education gathered research findings from 1982 to 2015 and found that moderate use of technology benefits student achievement (across all levels) when focusing on pedagogical aspects of applications delivered through adequately trained teachers.

Having said the above, the key challenge with selecting EdTech products is validating their efficacy in the context of their application and use. While there is an ever-increasing number of EdTech solutions, it is not always true that all existing or popular EdTech products actually benefit their users. For example, experts found, through an analysis of over 120 children's educational apps, that most did not align with core learning principles and had little educational value.

Because the efficacy of EdTech solutions depends on the context of the use, there is a need for EdTech products to be evaluated based on a holistic approach using a range of qualifiers appropriate for a given context. Qualifiers may be the existence of suitable infrastructure for the EdTech product to function, appropriate legal and policy frameworks, sufficient funding for deployment and maintenance, adequate national curriculum and delivery methods, teachers competent to use the EdTech product effectively, and supportive home and community environments for learners.

While there are many online sources that maintain repositories of promising EdTech products and solutions, just a few have been identified as the most reliable, accurate, categorically and geographically diverse, and up to date. These are EdTech Impact, EdSurge Product Index, Common Sense Education, and Education Alliance Finland. The EdTech solutions in these repositories have been systematically reviewed, analyzed, and categorized by type of offering. The report groups the EdTech solutions into three categories based on their functions and purposes: EdTech for Teaching and Learning, EdTech for Education Governance, and EdTech for Employability and Entrepreneurship. Each category has several subcategories that capture relevant types of EdTech solutions within that specific category.

By considering the categories of EdTech solutions, the Asian Development Bank (ADB) has developed a proprietary Quality, Effectiveness, Scalability, Affordability (QESA) EdTech Evaluation Framework, which makes the evaluation process systematic and sets transparent and fair criteria for EdTech providers. Key metrics of QESA assessment and selection framework areas are quality, evidence, sustainability, and affordability. The QESA toolkit helps education decision makers evaluate a potential technology-based solution using a set of questions and scoring rubric to naturally arrive at a decision by using the right metrics.

Research of best practices indicates that, for effective and appropriate use of EdTech to transform education, it is important to have a plan for implementation and utilization at scale. Based on previous research, two main principles have been proposed to guide this process.

1. Staged development is recommended for scaling EdTech, wherein countries implement digital solutions in stages rather than rushing into cutting-edge tools right away. This approach involves introducing, improving, and scaling utilization step-by-step.

2. Scaling EdTech systematically, instead of in siloes, involves addressing all areas that affect its use simultaneously, even if it means slower progress in a particular area.

Overall, for any given country for which EdTech scaling is being considered, low-tech, medium-tech, and high-tech approaches can be differentiated depending on the state of development of the national infrastructure, government, schools, teachers, learners, and technology and service providers. Historically, many development efforts in digital education have focused too narrowly on devices and connectivity, neglecting other important pillars.

To support application of the abovementioned principles, ADB developed the five-pillar Digital Education Readiness Framework (DERF), with an associated tool that systematically assesses a country's readiness for digital education by collecting and analyzing data on infrastructure, policies, curriculum, schools, teachers, students, parents, providers, etc., using publicly available sources, as well as conducting surveys with teachers, students, and other education stakeholders to fill in any knowledge gaps.

Reimagining education transformation that fully integrates technology requires a staged and systematic approach, a holistic EdTech strategy, and a robust and practical implementation guide. Achieving this requires strategic decision-making, strong leadership, and preparation at the national and local levels. Having ensured the enabling environment, digitalization of quality education processes can be effectively and sequentially scaled up, leading to true transformation.

Recommendations

- **Undertake a systematic assessment of digital education readiness of the education system of a country.** Determine the stage of development and key development areas (gaps) of the system by using ADB's DERF with an associated tool to systematically assess e-readiness across five pillars such as infrastructure, governments, schools and teachers, students and home environment, and EdTech providers.

- **Develop a strategy and a road map based on the systematic assessment of digital readiness and the potential of EdTech to drive change in corresponding areas, as well as categories of solutions available.** Start by understanding the potential of EdTech in enhancing education outcomes, followed by learning about the types (categories) of EdTech solutions available. Develop a strategy that systematically and holistically addresses the key problems and requirements in functional areas of EdTech such as teaching and learning, education governance, and employability and skills development.

- **Verify and validate efficacy of EdTech products and solutions prior to procurement decisions. Aim to address all areas that affect the use of EdTech simultaneously, taking a holistic and staged approach to sector development, and by selecting EdTech solutions best fit to the given country context using QESA EdTech Evaluation Framework and product evaluation toolkit**. In addition to reviewing the generic efficacy portfolio of a specific EdTech product, evaluate it using a range of qualifiers appropriate for a given context. The qualifiers include the availability of suitable (low-tech, medium-tech, high-tech) infrastructure for the product to function, appropriate legal and policy frameworks, sufficient funding for deployment and maintenance, adequate national curriculum and delivery methods, teachers competent to use the product effectively, and supportive home and community environments for learners. Devise an implementation plan based on the staged and systematic (holistic) development approach and QESA EdTech Evaluation Framework (along with the selection toolkit's guiding questions) to select the right solutions.

1 A Vision

Artificial intelligence (AI) and immersive learning technologies, such as augmented reality and virtual reality, are revolutionizing personalized adaptive learning. These advancements facilitate the shift from traditional teaching methods to a more student-centered approach. Teachers are now adopting roles as facilitators, coaches, and mentors, allowing for increased student engagement through digital instructional materials.[1]

These technologies enable individualized feedback and real-time assessments, as well as offering personalized learning paths based on students' interests, skills, and pace. Additionally, adaptive learning technologies allow for continuous monitoring of student progress, leading to improved outcomes. Furthermore, they can empower students to develop innovative solutions for real-world challenges such as climate change by fostering data-driven decision-making, promoting cross-disciplinary collaboration, and accelerating the creation of sustainable technologies.[2]

AI, machine learning, and adaptive learning technologies are disrupting the education sector by providing differentiated and individualized learning experiences. Virtual tutors and intelligent tutoring systems support personalized learning, while digital teaching assistants streamline time-consuming administrative tasks for teachers. This level of automation allows for better student guidance and increased teacher efficiency.

As an example, ChatGPT, an AI-driven technology by OpenAI, could revolutionize personalized adaptive learning. As an advanced language model, it aids educators in creating tailored content, offering instant feedback, and generating assessments.[3] By understanding context and generating human-like responses, ChatGPT fosters engaging learning environments and helps address individual student needs more effectively.

Adaptive learning technologies have the potential to enable personalized learning at scale, helping higher education institutions improve course success and reduce student withdrawal rates. Meanwhile, makerspaces and fab labs, equipped with tools like 3D printers and scanners, provide hands-on exploration and experimentation opportunities for students and inventors.

In sum, adaptive and immersive learning technologies are transforming teaching and learning, making truly personalized learning a reality. These technologies facilitate student-centered learning, promoting lifelong learning, and help expand educational opportunities across the globe.

---

[1] Asian Development Bank (ADB). 2019. *Leveraging Education Technology: Transformation of Teaching and Learning in Asia and the Pacific.* Manila.

[2] International Telecommunication Union (ITU). 2023. *AI for Good. 7 AI Innovations Helping to Combat Climate Change. Geneva.* https://aiforgood.itu.int/7-ai-innovations-helping-to-combat-climate-change/.

[3] G. Cooper. 2023. Examining Science Education in ChatGPT: An Exploratory Study of Generative Artificial Intelligence. *Journal of Science Education and Technology.* 32. pp. 444–452. https://link.springer.com/article/10.1007/s10956-023-10039-y.

2 Background

Education technology (EdTech) is broadly defined as the study and practice of facilitating learning and improving performance by creating, using and managing technological processes and resources.[4]

The vision described reflects the effective use of EdTech through immersive learning simulation, just one example of the pedagogical use of technology.[5] What may seem to most like a distant dream is achievable at scale with the digital transformation of education. While exploring opportunities to use cutting-edge technology to improve learning, it is important to underline the importance of foundational learning, as basic literacy and numeracy skills form the basis for transformational learning approaches.

The use of technology in education has increased over the years, but the evolution has not been free of trouble. Too often, new technologies have been introduced in resource-poor education environments with the expectation that information and communication technology (ICT) itself would catalyze much-needed changes in education systems.[6] Such failures have engendered distrust of EdTech.[7]

To prevent such failures, strategy should prioritize sound pedagogy, train educators to use technology effectively to support instruction, and build overall capacity.[8] While research suggests that the presence of technology improves student achievement, the best results are achieved with supplemental EdTech applications, not with truly transformational solutions.[9]

---

[4]   P. Mishra, M.J. Koehler, and K. Kereluik. 2009. Looking Back to the Future of Educational Technology. *TechTrends.* 53 (5). p. 49.

[5]   J.M. Beckem and M. Watkins. 2012. Bringing Life to Learning: Immersive Experiential Learning Simulations for Online and Blended Courses. *Journal of Asynchronous Learning Networks.* 16 (5). pp. 61–70.

[6]   S. Isaacs. 2013. Turning on Mobile Learning in Africa and the Middle East: Illustrative Initiatives and Policy Implications. *UNESCO Working Paper Series on Mobile Learning.* Paris: United Nations Educational, Scientific and Cultural Organization.

[7]   N. Kardaras. 2016. Screens in Schools Are a $60 Billion Hoax. *Time.* 31 August. https://time.com/4474496/screens-schools-hoax/.

[8]   UNESCO Institute for Statistics. 2016. ICT in Education Statistics: Shifting from Regional Reporting to Global Monitoring; Progress Made, Challenges Encountered, and the Way Forward. *UNESCO Global Education Monitoring Report.* Paris: United Nations Educational, Scientific and Cultural Organization.

[9]   R. Bernard et al. 2018. Gauging the Effectiveness of Educational Technology Integration in Education: What the Best-Quality Meta-Analyses Tell Us. DOI: 10.1007/978-3-319-17727-4_109-1.

The reasons for a lack of transformational use of technology are much debated, with some maintaining that the use of EdTech is heavily restricted by how education systems work.[10] One example of systematic limitation is the use of standardized testing to assess learners and decide whether they can advance to the next grade. When every student takes the same test at the same time, there is little incentive to use technology to make learning more personalized and adaptive to the student's level, even though these qualities are key to high-quality pedagogy. This leaves EdTech providers having to choose between developing truly transformational solutions or giving in to restrictions and building supplemental solutions that are only moderately effective in the current setup.[11]

Aims of This Report

Technological development is increasing rapidly, and new educational solutions spread to schools quickly, especially since the spread of coronavirus disease (COVID-19) and the resulting urgent need for remote learning. Education ministries are challenged to be timely in their efforts to measure progress and understand how best to benefit from EdTech with the tech-inclusive education approach, in which technology is fully integrated into digitalizing educational processes, and in their decisions about how to use technology in line with pedagogical choices, governance, and administrative processes involving all stakeholders.

With the theme of reimagining education, this report offers a comprehensive view of EdTech, resources with which to build a strategy and road map to reimagine tech-inclusive education, and supporting evidence.

This report seeks to

(i)   provide a topical update on the state of the digital transformation of education;

(ii)   argue for the use EdTech by reviewing evidence of its efficacy;

(iii) demonstrate what EdTech is by exploring its product landscape with representative examples; and

(iv)   define key areas to address to successfully implement EdTech in teaching and learning.

---

[10]   I. Alexander et al. 2021. *Tech-Inclusive Education: A World-Class System for Every Child*. Tony Blair Institute for Global Change. https://institute.global/policy/tech-inclusive-education-world-class-system-every-child.

[11]   O. Vallo. 2022. *Is Efficacy Research Killing EdTech Innovation?* EdTech Digest Column. https://www.edtechdigest.com/2022/07/05/is-efficacy-research-killing-edtech-innovation/.

Learning Crisis

EdTech has become more popular in the past couple of decades because current school systems are unable to provide affordable, high-quality learning at scale. Research has found that children come out of school with large deficits in foundational literacy and numeracy skills.[12] Globally, the learning crisis disproportionately affects the poorest countries, where seven out of 10 children will not learn basic primary school skills (Figure 1).

Figure 1: Global Learning Crisis

A global learning crisis: The expected learning outcomes of the cohort of children and youth who are of school age in 2030

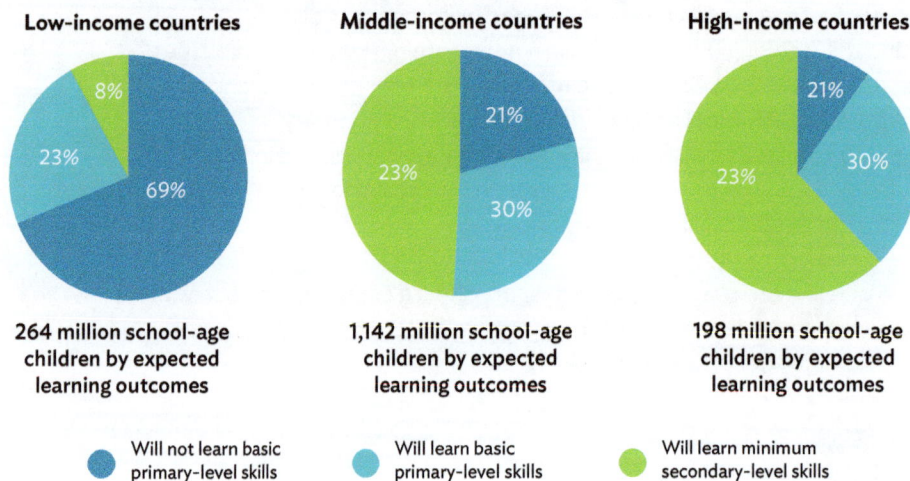

Low-income countries

8%
23%
69%

264 million school-age children by expected learning outcomes

Middle-income countries

21%
23%
30%

1,142 million school-age children by expected learning outcomes

High-income countries

21%
30%
23%

198 million school-age children by expected learning outcomes

● Will not learn basic primary-level skills   ● Will learn basic primary-level skills   ● Will learn minimum secondary-level skills

Source: Education Commission. 2016. *The Learning Generation: Investing in Education for a Changing World*. New York.

In addition to deficient learning outcomes, another issue is the number of school dropouts, which worsened under the COVID-19 pandemic. A forecasted 84 million school-age children will be out of school in 2030, with only one in six countries close to having at least 95% of their youth completing secondary school. In that year, fewer than two in three children are expected to achieve minimal skills and complete primary school, leaving 300 million people without these skills.[13]

The poorest children often suffer the most from the many barriers that prevent their education. Many living in rural areas find it a challenge or impossible to get to school every day. In economically challenging times, children in disadvantaged families

---

[12]   World Bank. 2018. *Growing Smarter: Learning and Equitable Development in East Asia and Pacific*. Washington, DC. https://elibrary.worldbank.org/doi/abs/10.1596/978-1-4648-1261-3.

[13]   UNESCO Institute for Statistics. 2022. *Setting Commitments: National SDG 4 Benchmarks to Transform Education*. Paris: United Nations Educational, Scientific and Cultural Organization. https://www.unesco.org/gem-report/en/2022-sdg4-benchmarks.

may have to work to provide for their families. The United Nations Children's Fund (UNICEF) estimated that 44% of girls and 34% of boys in the poorest quintile either drop out of primary school or never start (Figure 2).

The magnitude of the challenge renders incremental change inadequate. As hundreds of millions of students do not acquire even the most foundational skills, significantly better ways are needed to deliver high-quality education at scale.

Figure 2: Educational Status of Poorest Quintile Adolescents (ages 10–19 years)

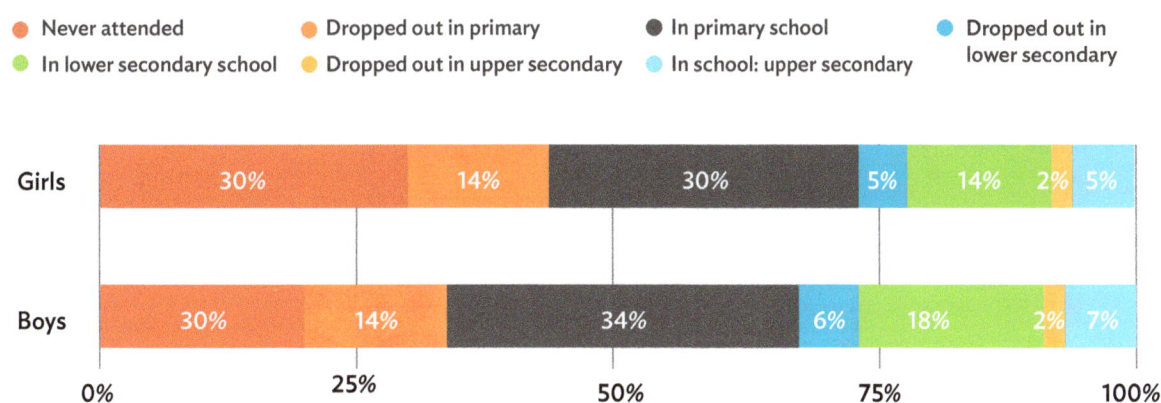

Educational status of poorest quintile adolescents (ages 10–19 years)

- Never attended
- Dropped out in primary
- In primary school
- Dropped out in lower secondary
- In lower secondary school
- Dropped out in upper secondary
- In school: upper secondary

Girls	30%	14%	30%	5%	14%	2%	5%
Boys	30%	14%	34%	6%	18%	2%	7%

0%   25%   50%   75%   100%

Source: A. Imchen and F. Ndem. 2020. *Addressing the Learning Crisis: An Urgent Need to Better Finance Education for the Poorest Children.* UNICEF. https://www.unicef.org/media/63896/file/Addressing-the-learning-crisis-advocacy-brief-2020.pdf.

Remediating Learning Loss

In addition to addressing the learning crisis, education systems must remediate learning losses incurred under the pandemic. The duration of school closure varied among countries, but, on average, two-thirds of an academic year were lost worldwide in 2020 and 2021 as schools were unable to operate.[14] By July 2022, schools had been partly or fully closed for an average of 38 weeks globally because of the pandemic, with India and Indonesia the worst affected in Asia and the Pacific (Figure 3).

Widespread school closure inevitably brought large learning losses. Schools have now largely reopened, but student learning will not recover fully without strategically implemented action. For many children, schools provide more than structured learning, offering key support as well for health, nutrition, and general well-being. School closures thus have far-reaching effects in addition to learning loss.

---

[14]   J.S. Chanduvi et al. 2022. *Where Are We on Education Recovery?* UNICEF.

Figure 3: The Length of Full and Partial School Closures in Asia during the Pandemic

Full and partial school closures in Asia (in years)

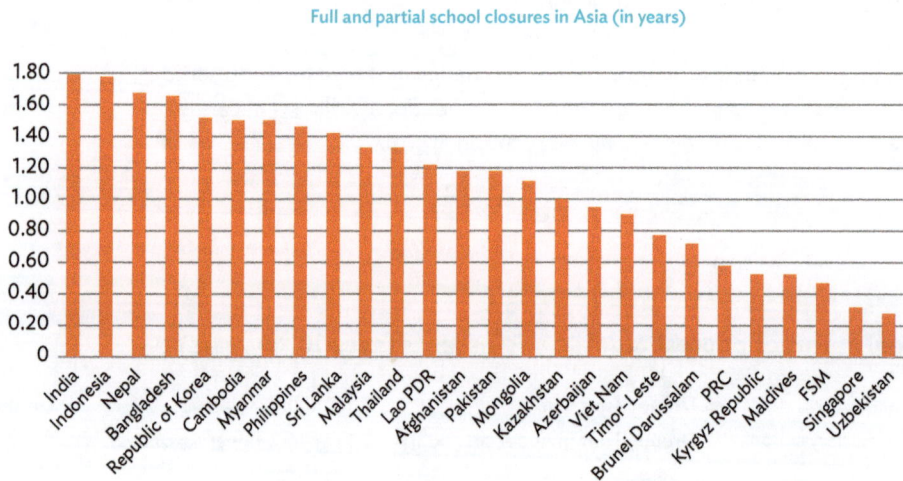

FSM = Federated States of Micronesia, Lao PDR = Lao People's Democratic Republic, PRC = People's Republic of China.
Source: UNESCO Global monitoring of school closures caused by COVID-19 (2022).

Recovery programs will vary between countries, but UNICEF suggests five key actions for education recovery (footnote 14):

(i) **Reach and retain.** Track the number of children who are back in school.

(ii) **Assess.** Measure students' current learning levels.

(iii) **Prioritize.** Adjust curricula to focus on fundamentals.

(iv) **Increase.** Implement remediation and catch-up programs at scale to address learning losses.

(v) **Develop.** Provide additional measures for children's well-being.

The effective use of EdTech is integral to learning recovery strategies, especially in remote and self-directed learning. UNICEF and the World Bank have therefore created a set of seven resource packs to help government officials explore effective remote learning opportunities using print, television, radio, digital technology, and mobile phones.[15] The variety of approaches reveals the diversity of recovery mechanisms to be used, depending on a country's digital education readiness.

An ADB brief outlines two main approaches to using EdTech to support recovery. First, EdTech can provide feedback loops for assessing students' individual learning levels, and then provide lessons tailored to each learner's skill level. Second, EdTech can enable effective formative assessment to gauge student progress and measure how effective learning recovery strategies are in the classroom.[16]

---

[15] UNICEF and World Bank. 2022. *Remote Learning Packs.* Washington, DC. https://inee.org/resources/remote-learning-packs.

[16] R. Molato-Gayares et al. 2022. *How to Recover Learning Losses from COVID-19 School Closures in Asia and the Pacific. ADB Briefs.* No. 217. Manila: Asian Development Bank. http://dx.doi.org/10.22617/BRF220301-2.

Skill Gap Challenge

Rapid technological advances are disrupting the workplace. Jobs that involve repetitive tasks or those that can be easily codified are more likely to be automated. This includes jobs in manufacturing, data entry, and some service industries.[17] In Southeast Asia, more than half of the combined workforce of 137 million in Cambodia, Indonesia, the Philippines, Thailand, and Viet Nam are at risk of displacement by robots, particularly in the garment manufacturing industry.[18] ADB estimated that 5%–28% of all jobs are at high risk of loss in a selection of regional economies (Figure 4).

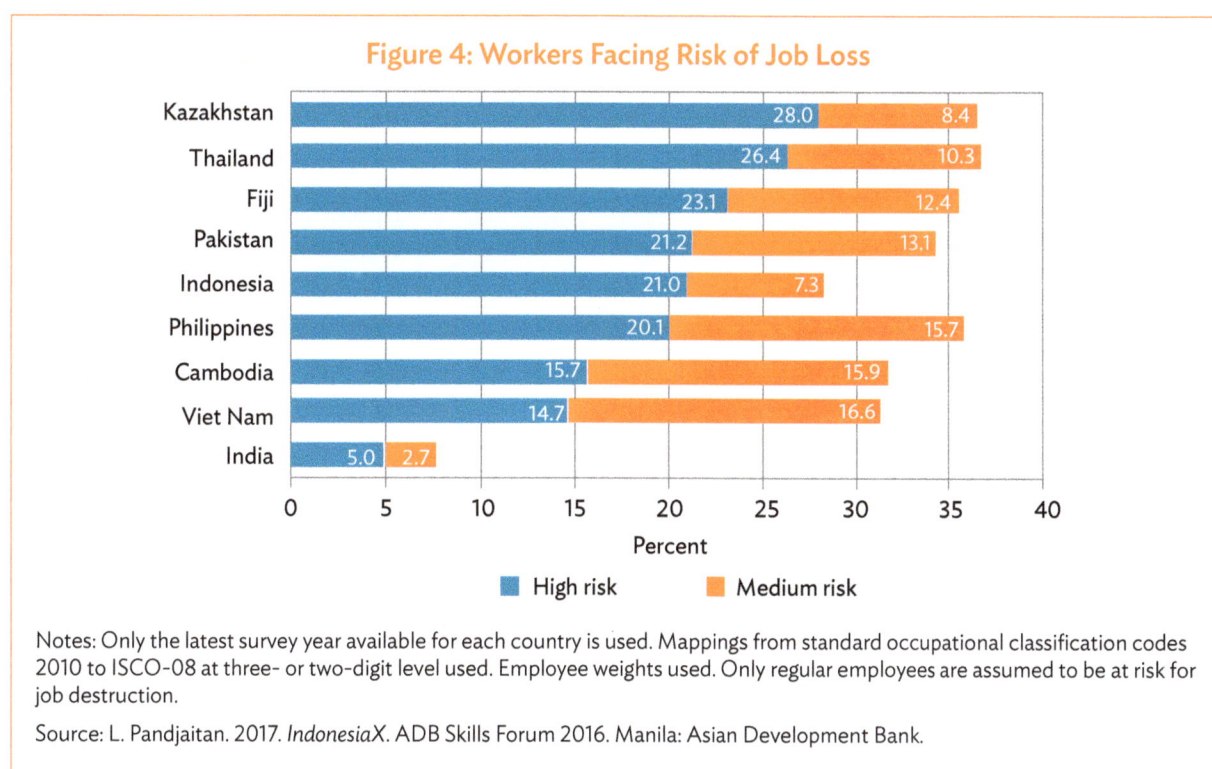

Figure 4: Workers Facing Risk of Job Loss

Notes: Only the latest survey year available for each country is used. Mappings from standard occupational classification codes 2010 to ISCO-08 at three- or two-digit level used. Employee weights used. Only regular employees are assumed to be at risk for job destruction.

Source: L. Pandjaitan. 2017. *IndonesiaX*. ADB Skills Forum 2016. Manila: Asian Development Bank.

Preparing for the jobs of tomorrow will require workers to have a robust skill set with technological, higher-order cognitive and behavioral skills underpinned by strong foundational skills developed through solid primary and secondary education. A new generation of 21st century skills fall into three core categories: foundational literacy, occupational competency, and character quality. Surveys in several countries reveal that employers value skills such as communication, collaboration, problem-solving, and critical thinking as highly as specialized occupational skills.[19] Wider use

---

[17]   World Bank Group. 2016. *World Development Report 2016: Digital Dividends*. Washington, DC: World Bank Publications.

[18]   J.-H. Chang and P. Huynh. 2016. ASEAN in Transformation: The Future of Jobs at Risk of Automation. *Bureau for Employers' Activities Working Paper*. No. 9. Geneva: International Labour Organization. http://www.ilo.org/actemp/publications/WCMS_579554/lang--en/index.htm.

[19]   World Bank. 2018. *Growing Smarter: Learning and Equitable Development in East Asia and Pacific*. Washington, DC. https://elibrary.worldbank.org/doi/abs/10.1596/978-1-4648-1261-3.

of educational technology can help learners to develop these skills in several ways. For example, it can provide opportunities for collaboration and communication by enabling students to work on projects together, regardless of their location. Furthermore, according to Loveless (2002),[20] technology facilitates creative learning experiences in schools that include developing ideas, creating and making, collaboration, and communication and evaluation.

Education systems must respond to the changing needs of society by teaching the skills necessary for work and good citizenship. Digital environments have become omnipresent, and people need the basic competency that enables their safe, healthy, effective, and appropriate use.

---

[20]   A. Loveless. 2002. Literature Review in Creativity, New Technologies and Learning. Volume 4 of NESTA *Futurelab Series report*. NESTA Futurelab.

3   What Is EdTech?

EdTech combines hardware, software, and research-based practices to improve traditional education methods. EdTech is a fast-moving, multibillion-dollar global industry that has the potential to transform education for good. It is also a pedagogical tool that helps learners, educators, and education sector stakeholders to improve practices.

When comparing EdTech with traditional educational materials such as paper textbooks, the product offering is vast, innovative, and diverse. Whereas textbook content creation, editing, publishing, and distribution are mainly conducted by a handful of major publishing houses, the EdTech sector features thousands of small and midsized start-ups globally. The barrier to entry is low in EdTech, as anyone with adequate technical and design skills can create a learning app and sell it online. This enriches the variety of learning innovations but also makes it difficult for EdTech users and buyers to discern the highest-quality and most suitable products from the many competitors on offer.

EdTech products encompass a range of applications, among them learning management systems (LMSs), mobile learning apps, massive online open courses, assessment platforms, and quiz tools. When used well, the best of these tools can be transformational, but to truly benefit from EdTech requires an understanding of the wider educational ecosystem.

EdTech Offerings

Current EdTech products on offer reveal technology's role in education transformation. A wide selection of online EdTech product repositories typically include product reviews and feature listings, which can help locate products for specific purposes. Repositories categorize solutions based on different criteria such as features and functions, target audiences, or pricing models, either free or not.

Often, EdTech pricing models depend on whether the solution is created by a commercial firm or a nonprofit organization. For free and low-cost solutions, open educational resources and open-source software are available in the public domain.[21] The most popular open-source EdTech solutions include the LMS Moodle (https://moodle.org/) and the education management system OpenEMIS (https://www.openemis.org/). To narrow the digital divide, the United Nations Educational, Scientific and Cultural Organization (UNESCO) offers support in using open educational resources.

---

[21]   Institute for the Study of Knowledge Management in Education. 2022. *OER Commons Platform.* https://www.oercommons.org/.

While open-source software and open educational resources can be accessed freely, implementation often requires funding for server costs, staff time, training, and maintenance, illustrating that there is always a cost for implementing EdTech. The best return on investment requires a careful process of curating the most suitable solutions.

EdTech Product Landscape

When implementing EdTech, it is important to consider "Why" before "What" because technology should serve a pedagogical purpose and support learning objectives and should never be used for technology's sake.

Starting with the "Why" allows educators to ensure that technology use is aligned with their objectives and enhances learning. By first considering outcomes and problems, teachers can then determine and select the appropriate technology. This approach ensures that technology is used effectively and efficiently. However, to effectively assess the potential benefits of EdTech, it is important to form a general understanding of the product landscape and what proven benefits different types of solutions can provide for learners.

An EdTech product taxonomy organizes solutions in three categories (Figure 5) based on their functions and purposes:

(i)   EdTech for Teaching and Learning,
(ii)   EdTech for Education Governance, and
(iii)   EdTech for Employability and Entrepreneurship.

Figure 5: Three Major Categories of EdTech Products

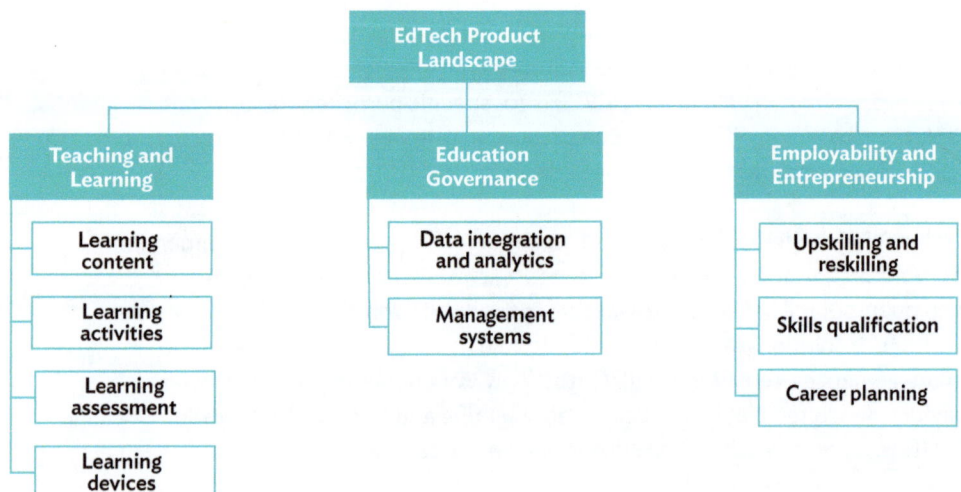

EdTech = education technology.
Source: Teaching and Learning EdTech product categorization (ADB 2022).

The characteristics of each category are defined by benefits, as confirmed by research. For benefits to be realized, the solution needs to align with learning science principles.

The teaching and learning category includes products and devices used for instruction and improving pedagogy and assessment practices (Figure 6). These include products that come with off-the-shelf content, activities, and assessment that the educator can tailor as needed.

Figure 6: Category 1: EdTech for Teaching and Learning

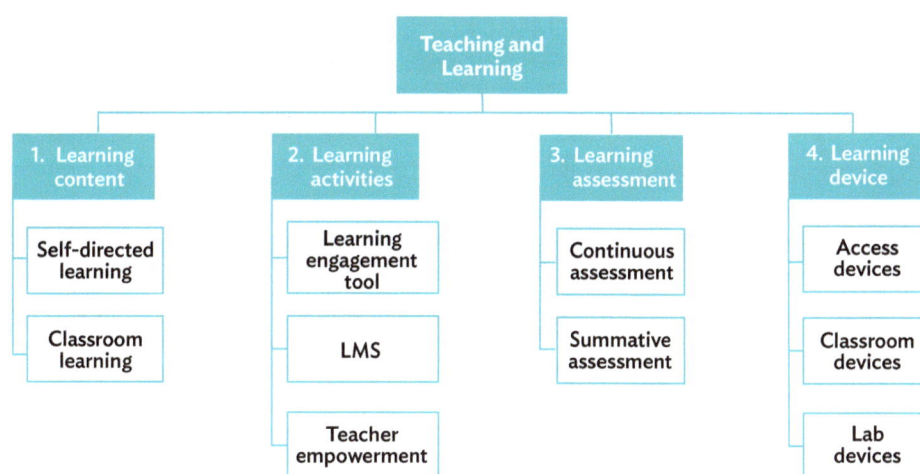

Teaching and Learning

1. Learning content
- Self-directed learning
- Classroom learning

2. Learning activities
- Learning engagement tool
- LMS
- Teacher empowerment

3. Learning assessment
- Continuous assessment
- Summative assessment

4. Learning device
- Access devices
- Classroom devices
- Lab devices

EdTech = education technology, LMS = learning management system.
Source: Teaching and Learning EdTech product categorization (ADB 2022).

For classroom instruction and supporting the development of conceptual understanding of complex topics such as chemical reactions or how bonds between atoms are formed or broken, these solutions can offer explanations and analysis using rich multimedia. Dynamic visualizations and simulations can help students conceptualize many subjects. A significant amount of research has demonstrated the effectiveness of EdTech simulations.[22]

Another benefit of EdTech is its ability to provide timely and continuous feedback at scale, which many teachers struggle with, especially with large classes. Feedback on learning becomes less useful as response time increases.[23] Some EdTech tools allow automated feedback by offering learners the opportunity to monitor and regulate their own performance. Students' intrinsic motivation to complete the task increases, as does their confidence.[24] Continuous feedback can drive engagement and higher

---

[22] A. Widiyatmoko. 2018. The Effectiveness of Simulation in Science Learning on Conceptual Understanding: A Literature Review. *Journal of International Development and Cooperation.* 24 (1). pp. 35–43.

[23] A. Irons and S. Elkington. 2021. *Enhancing Learning through Formative Assessment and Feedback.* Abingdon: Routledge.

[24] H. Schaap. 2011. "Students" Personal Professional Theories in Vocational Education: Developing a Knowledge Base. PhD dissertation. Utrecht University.

completion rates in mathematics, literacy, language learning, and other subjects in which progress comes through practice.

The third advantage of EdTech is its ability to personalize learning through customization based on learner skills, prior knowledge, abilities, preferences, and background. A meta-analysis of 16 randomized controlled trials in five countries found technology-supported personalized learning to have a statistically significant positive effect. Personalized approaches that adapt or adjust to the learners' level had a significantly greater impact than those linked only to learners' interests by providing personalized feedback, support, and/or assessment.[25]

Access devices are hardware used by students and teachers to access digital resources, such as LMSs, digital textbooks, and online educational tools. Examples include laptops, tablets, and smartphones.

Classroom devices consist of school-based hardware, such as interactive whiteboards, projectors, computers, and document cameras. Classroom devices help teachers engage students and create interactive learning experiences. They also make it easier for teachers to deliver digital content and collaborate with students.

Lab devices include specialized hardware, such as scientific experiments, engineering projects, and creative work. Examples include virtual reality headsets, 3D printers, robotics kits, and scientific sensors.

Figure 7: Category 2: EdTech for Education Governance

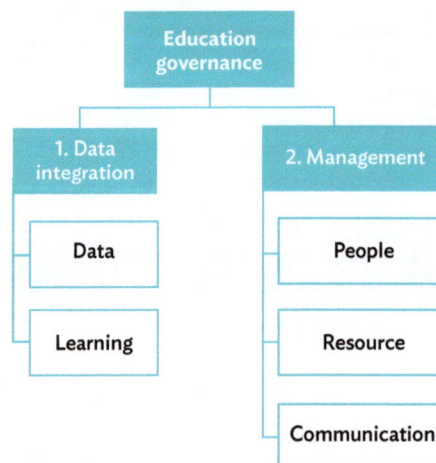

EdTech = education technology.
Source: Teaching and Learning EdTech product categorization (ADB 2022).

---

[25] L. Major, G.A. Francis, and M. Tsapali. 2021. The Effectiveness of Technology-Supported Personalised Learning in Low- and Middle-Income Countries: A Meta-Analysis. *British Journal of Educational Technology*. 52 (5). pp. 1935–1964.

Education governance products are used to manage resources and people, integrate data, analyze learning, and communicate effectively (Figure 7). They improve the efficiency and/or transparency of processes.

When the number of EdTech tools in use increases, it is important to manage user licenses, credentials, and data. Platforms that offer data interoperability have thus become more popular, as they allow easy access and management and facilitate privacy. Research suggests that a coherent environment is needed to fully exploit the possibilities of EdTech to collect, store, and utilize data for learners' benefit. This requires a local, regional, or national system in which data are collected and used to inform teachers, parents, and students about learning progress, and to inform decisions about curriculum and technology adoption.[26]

Education management information systems (EMISs) are digital platforms used by education administrators, managers, and staff such as teachers to facilitate decision-making; oversee administrative tasks; and manage pupils, financial resources, human resources, and learning data. A high-quality EMIS is useful for teaching and learning as well as for planning and policy.

Much of the increased use of EdTech is for enterprise resource planning (ERP), i.e., spending on devices, training, connectivity, content, and other facilities. ERP enhances the ability of colleges, schools, and departments to teach and research at a reasonable or low cost.[27] A key benefit of ERP is its improved access to accurate and timely information.

Employability and entrepreneurship products are used for career planning, skill qualification, and professional development (Figure 8). As noted earlier, demand in the job market continually changes with digitalization and automation, and as climate change requires that the education sector transition to a green economy by preparing green skills, defined as "the knowledge, abilities, values, and attitudes needed to live in, develop and support a sustainable and resource-efficient society."[28]

By 2025, an estimated 85 million jobs globally may be displaced as an estimated 97 million new roles emerge.[29] A 2021 McKinsey report predicted that one-quarter of the United States (US) workforce is at risk of being replaced by automation.[30] Factory workers, office clerks, and administrative secretaries are generally mentioned as roles that are likely to become automated. A shift toward a green economy also has a strong influence on the job market, with the International Labour Organization estimating in 2018 that 24 million jobs worldwide could be created by the green economy by 2030.[31] While forecasts of future job markets vary, there is a strong

26   K.L. Best and J.F. Pane. 2018. *Privacy and Interoperability Challenges Could Limit the Benefits of Education Technology*. RAND Corporation.
27   E.E. Watson and H. Schneider. 1999. Using ERP Systems in Education. *Communications of the Association for Information Systems*. 1 (1). p. 9.
28   Cedefop. 2012. European Centre for the Development of Vocational Training. http://www.cedefop.europa.eu.
29   World Economic Forum. 2020. *The Future of Jobs Report 2020*. Geneva.
30   S. Lund et al. 2021. *The Future of Work after COVID-19*. McKinsey Global Institute.
31   International Labour Organization. 2018. *World Employment Social Outlook 2018: Greening with Jobs*. Geneva.

Figure 8: Category 3: EdTech for Employability and Entrepreneurship

```
                      ┌─────────────────────┐
                      │  Employability and  │
                      │   entrepreneurship  │
                      └─────────────────────┘
        ┌───────────────────────┼───────────────────────┐
┌─────────────────┐    ┌─────────────────┐    ┌─────────────────┐
│ 1. Upskilling and│    │ 2. Skills       │    │ 3. Career       │
│    reskilling    │    │    qualification│    │    planning     │
└─────────────────┘    └─────────────────┘    └─────────────────┘
   ┌─────────────┐        ┌─────────────┐        ┌─────────────┐
   │Self-directed│        │  Assessment │        │ Data-informed│
   │  learning   │        │             │        │decision making│
   └─────────────┘        └─────────────┘        └─────────────┘
   ┌─────────────┐        ┌─────────────┐        ┌─────────────┐
   │Institutional│        │ Credentialing│       │Mentoring/guidance│
   └─────────────┘        └─────────────┘        └─────────────┘
```

EdTech = education technology.
Source: Teaching and Learning EdTech product categorization (ADB 2022).

consensus that tens of millions of current jobs are going to disappear while new jobs and forms of work appear.

With recent changes in the labor market, upskilling and reskilling have been on the rise. Upskilling is learning new skills to supplement existing competencies, while reskilling helps workers acquire new skills to do a new job. A notable 36% of EdTech unicorns—companies valued at over $1 billion—provide upskilling and reskilling solutions.[32] Learners use upskilling and reskilling platforms throughout the workforce cycle. Students can use the platforms to supplement coursework, access offerings otherwise unavailable to them, and prepare to transition from academia to employment. Adult learners can use upskilling platforms on the job as part of a corporate learning and development program in parallel with their work or job search, to prevent skill erosion, and to stay relevant in the job market.[33]

Besides upskilling and reskilling, EdTech can enhance career planning through data utilization, assessments, tutoring, and learning plans. Higher education career services have adopted EdTech to streamline processes, collect data, and provide career and employability information resources.[34]

---

[32] HolonIQ. 2022. Global EdTech Unicorns. *The Complete List of Global EdTech Unicorns.* https://www.holoniq. com/edtech-unicorns.

[33] A. Lands and C. Pasha. 2021. Reskill to Rebuild: Coursera's Global Partnership with Government to Support Workforce Recovery at Scale. In S. Ra, S. Jagannathan, and R. Maclean, eds. *Powering a Learning Society during an Age of Disruption.* Singapore: Springer.

[34] E. Knight, T. Staunton, and M. Healy. 2022. About University Career Services' Interaction with EdTech. *Digital Transformation and Disruption of Higher Education.* 303.

4 Why Use EdTech?

The reasons for implementing EdTech are twofold. First, there is an urgent need to significantly improve education. According to UNESCO, achieving Sustainable Development Goal 4 (SDG 4) for high-quality education depends on exploiting the opportunities posed by technology. Six of 10 SDG 4 targets involve the use of technology in education. Second, students need to understand and be able to use technology. According to UNESCO, technology in schools affects education through five distinct channels: input, means of delivery, skill, tool for planning, and provider of a social and cultural context.[35]

Evidence of EdTech Efficacy

Technology's role in education has been a topic of research since it started to make its way to classrooms and learning practices, and the field is very diverse. The main challenge is to discover how technology is used to play a major role in determining outcomes. As a result, it can be more informative to examine specific pedagogical benefits, rather than looking at overall results.

When looking at EdTech efficacy, only the most recent research reveals more positive outcomes when broken down across generations of technology applications. In 2017, the National Bureau of Economic Research analyzed three distinct waves of research mapping the trajectory of technology-based approaches in EdTech over the past 2 decades (Figure 9).

Among the three generations of learning with EdTech, the third generation—from 2014 to 2018, during which blended learning approaches evolved—demonstrated the most positive impact on learning outcomes if implemented well.[36]

A review of 20 meta-analyses of EdTech effectiveness from K–12 to higher education gathered research findings from 1982 to 2015 (Figure 9). The three key findings on how EdTech affects learning are illustrated in Figure 10.

---

[35] Global Education Monitoring Report Team. 2021. Concept Note for the 2023 Global Education Monitoring Report on Technology and Education. Paris: UNESCO. https://unesdoc.unesco.org/ark:/48223/pf0000378950.

[36] M. Escueta et al. 2017. *Education Technology: An Evidence-Based Review. National Bureau of Economic Research.* https://docs.edtechhub.org/lib/AEIV8XGY.

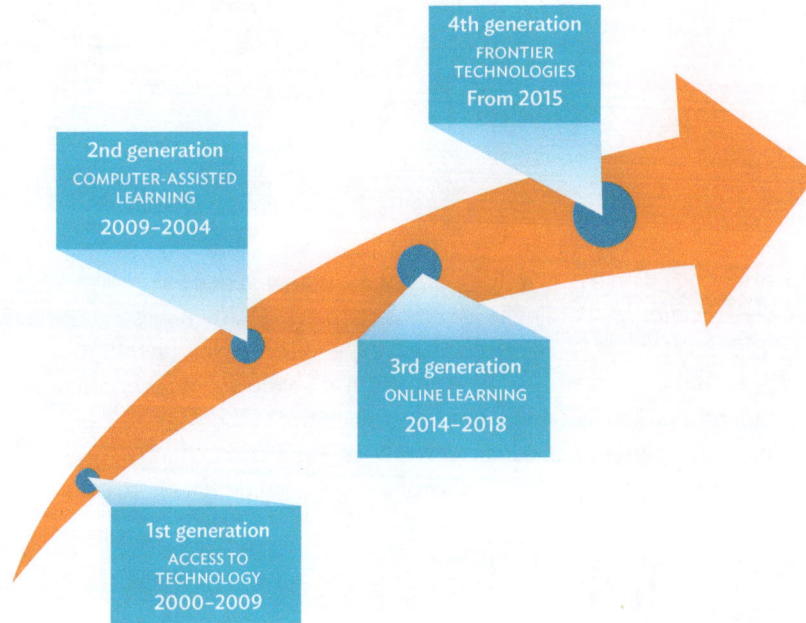

Figure 9: Impact of Technology on Learning

4th generation
FRONTIER TECHNOLOGIES
From 2015

2nd generation
COMPUTER-ASSISTED LEARNING
2009–2004

3rd generation
ONLINE LEARNING
2014–2018

1st generation
ACCESS TO TECHNOLOGY
2000–2009

EdTech = education technology.

Source: R. Bernard et al. 2018. *Gauging the Effectiveness of Educational Technology Integration in Education: What the Best-Quality Meta-Analyses Tell Us.* DOI: 10.1007/978-3-319-17727-4_109-1.

Figure 10: Effects of EdTech in Learning

"The presence of technology is of benefit to student achievement. This benefit extens from elementary to graduate school education."

"The most essential finding is the importance of various pedagogical aspects of technology use and the importance of teacher training to use technology."

"The moderate use of technology has been shown to outweigh technology applications featuring all of the bells and whistles."

EdTech = education technology.

Source: R. Bernard et al. 2018. *Gauging the Effectiveness of Educational Technology Integration in Education: What the Best-Quality Meta-Analyses Tell Us.* DOI: 10.1007/978-3-319-17727-4_109-1.

Challenges to Measuring Efficacy

Clear evidence of enhanced learning outcomes, help for teachers' time management, or improved student engagement exists for very few EdTech tools, and no single EdTech solution can achieve the same result everywhere.[37] As mentioned, results depend on how the technology is used in classrooms, which is affected by several systemic factors such as policies, infrastructure, support for users, etc.

Because EdTech efficacy depends on the context of the use, there is a need for products to be evaluated with a holistic approach using a range of qualifiers appropriate for a given context. Qualifiers may be the existence of suitable infrastructure for the EdTech product to function, appropriate legal and policy frameworks, sufficient funding for deployment and maintenance, adequate national curriculum and delivery methods, teachers competent to use the product effectively, and supportive home and community environments for learners.

Toward measuring EdTech efficacy, ADB has developed the Digital Education Readiness Framework (DERF), with five pillars of digital learning: (i) infrastructure, (ii) governance and policy, (iii) schools and teachers, (iv) students and parents, and (v) EdTech providers. Each pillar influences the learning environment and consequently affects the outcomes achieved with an EdTech tool.[38] Together, the pillars encompass everything that affects the effectiveness of the EdTech product.

Types of Evidence

Because the learning environment is difficult to control, it is often prohibitively expensive and challenging to implement randomized controlled trials to test EdTech's efficacy. Such trials are standard in medical research and would offer the strongest evidence of EdTech efficacy; in their absence, various other kinds of evidence can provide more generalizable results that are still valid.

To understand the value of the different types of efficacy measurements, the US Department of Education has defined, as part of the Every Student Succeeds Act (ESSA), four tiers of evidence that schools should look at before procuring EdTech products (Table 1).).[39] Chicago Public Schools include a question in their standard request for information from EdTech vendors asking them to show that their solution has an evidence base aligned with ESSA. Similarly, the Los Angeles Unified School District requests its providers to show their evidence, along with data on and analysis of their solutions' impact.[40]

---

[37] A. Ganimian et al. 2020. *Realizing the Promise: How Can Education Technology Improve Learning for All.* Brookings Institution.

[38] Economist Impact. 2022. *The Digital Education Readiness Framework.*

[39] Institute of Education Sciences. 2015. What Works Clearinghouse: *Using the WWC To Find ESSA Tiers of Evidence.* Washington, DC. https://ies.ed.gov/ncee/wwc/essa.

[40] REL Midwest. 2019. ESSA *Tiers of Evidence What You Need to Know.* Regional Educational Laboratory at American Institutes for Research. Washington, DC. https://ies.ed.gov/ncee/edlabs/regions/midwest/pdf/blogs/RELMW-ESSA-Tiers-Video-Handout-508.pdf.

Table 1: Understanding the ESSA Tiers of Evidence

UNDERSTANDING THE ESSA TIERS OF EVIDENCE

	TIER 1 Strong evidence	TIER 2 Moderate evidence	TIER 3 Promising evidence	TIER 4 Demonstrates a Rationale
Study design	Well-designed and implemented experimental study, meets WWC standards without reservation	Well-designed and implemented quasi-experimental study meets WWC standard with reservations	Well-designed and implemented correlational study, statisticall controls for selection bias	Well-defined logic model based on rigorous research
Results of the Study	Statistically significant positive effect on a relevant outcome	Statistically significant positive effect on a relevant outcome	Statistically significant positive effect on a relevant outcome	An effort to study the effects of the intervention is planned or currently under way
Finding from related studies	No strong negative finding from experimental or quasi-experimental studies	No strong negative finding from experimental or quasi-experimental studies	No strong negative finding from experimental or quasi-experimental studies	N/A
Sample size and setting	At least 350 participants, conducted in more than one district or school	At least 350 participants, conducted in more than one district or school	N/A	N/A
Match	Similar population and setting to your setting	Similar population and setting to your setting	N/A	N/A

ESSA = Every Student Succeeds Act, N/A = not applicable, WWC = What Works Clearinghouse.

Source: REL Midwest. 2019. *ESSA Tiers of Evidence What You Need to Know.* Washington, DC: Regional Educational Laboratory at American Institutes for Research. https://ies.ed.gov/ncee/edlabs/regions/midwest/pdf/blogs/RELMW-ESSA-Tiers-Video-Handout-508.pdf.

5 How to Scale EdTech

Successful education transformation with EdTech hinges on using digital learning solutions effectively and appropriately. This report has so far described evidence-based benefits of EdTech and the product landscape. In this section, it guides the planning and implementation of digital learning. We propose two main principles for EdTech implementation and utilization at scale.

Staged Development

The first principle for scaling EdTech is to implement it in stages. Countries ought not rush into cutting-edge tools right from the start; instead, they should introduce, improve, and scale EdTech utilization step-by-step. Digital solutions that do not require student onboarding are easier to adopt since it is not obligatory to have devices for students, low connectivity is not an issue, and students do not have to register to a new solution. Such tools can help teachers in lesson preparation and in making lessons more interactive and illustrative. Examples include quiz tools, interactive whiteboards, and solutions to demonstrate nature phenomenon when teaching science, technology, engineering, and mathematics (STEM) subjects. Platforms that help teachers in lesson preparation and assessment can also save time, but require less work to get started with. Once a strong routine in using teacher-led EdTech solutions is built, it is easier to proceed in using more student-centered applications and technically more advanced tools.

Systematic Development

Second, we recommend scaling EdTech systematically, instead of in siloes. Addressing all areas that affect the use of EdTech simultaneously is best, even if it means slower progress on a particular area. The following five areas to be addressed are identified in ADB's DERF: (i) infrastructure, (ii) governance and policy, (iii) schools and teachers, (iv) students and parents, and (v) EdTech providers (footnote 38).

As an example, schools should not invest heavily in devices unless there is a proper internet connection, good quality digital content and solutions available, and resources to ensure that teachers and students can use the digital solutions in a pedagogically purposeful way.

As illustrated in Figure 11, the five dimensions are interconnected; therefore, there is a need to address equally the issues and challenges that arise from each dimension.

Figure 11: Siloed vs Balanced Approach to Education Sector Development

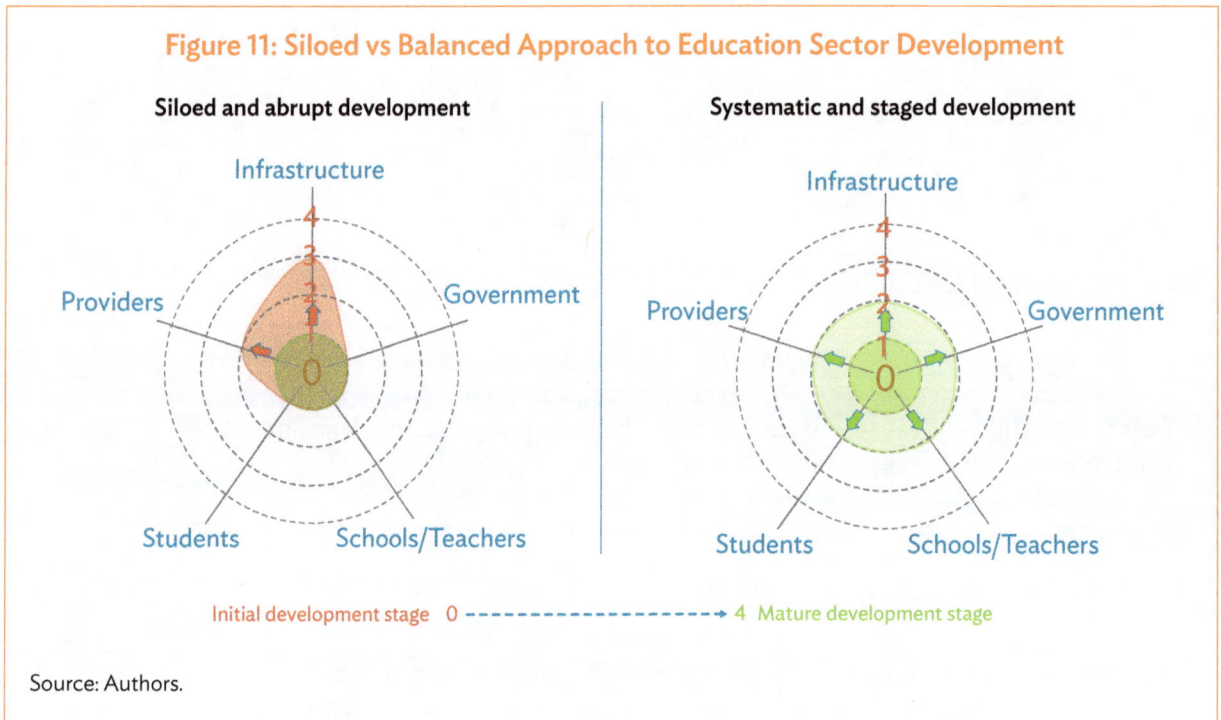

Siloed and abrupt development

Systematic and staged development

Initial development stage   0 - - - - - - - - - - - - - - - → 4   Mature development stage

Source: Authors.

Scaling EdTech in stages and systematically happens best through the following three intertwined stages:

(i)   assessment of digital education readiness,

(ii)   development of a holistic strategy, and

(iii)   implementation.

Assessing the Current State: Digital Education Readiness Framework

The current state of an education system sets the baseline for development toward a system in which EdTech improves learning quality and equity. An assessment of the current state needs to address five pillars that enable digital transformation (Figure 12).

The five critical pillars are based on ADB's DERF: "DERF has been built on the premise that progress in each of the five pillars is equally critical for a well-functioning digital education ecosystem, but infrastructure and policy are key foundational levers that accelerate progress across other areas (footnote 38)."

Addressing each of the five pillars is important because the scope of development efforts has often been too narrow, for example, focusing only on devices and

Figure 12: Five Pillars That Enable Digital Transformation

EdTech = education technology.

Source: Economist Impact. 2022. *The Digital Education Readiness Framework*.

connectivity, with other pillars neglected.[41] In such cases, technology has not been effective for lack of proper educational content and competency to use the technology.

The DERF project included, in its first phase, an assessment of readiness for digital education in 10 ADB developing member countries: Bangladesh, Cambodia, Fiji, Indonesia, the Kyrgyz Republic, Mongolia, Pakistan, the Philippines, Uzbekistan, and Viet Nam (footnote 38). The findings can be explored using the following:

- a web-based system that allows regional and cross-country comparison;
- a monitoring tool that incorporates time, place, and visualization of data; and
- the DERF.

Digital Education Readiness Framework. Readiness assessment involves collecting publicly available data on infrastructure, education, curriculum, and education policies. To fill in some information gaps, it is useful to conduct surveys with teachers, students, and other education stakeholders. The DERF categories in Figure 13 are a guideline for designing a country-wide readiness assessment.

---

41 OECD. 2015. Students, Computers and Learning: Making the Connection. Programme for International Student Assessment report. Paris: OECD Publishing. https://doi.org/10.1787/9789264239555-en.

Figure 13: Digital Education Readiness Framework Categories

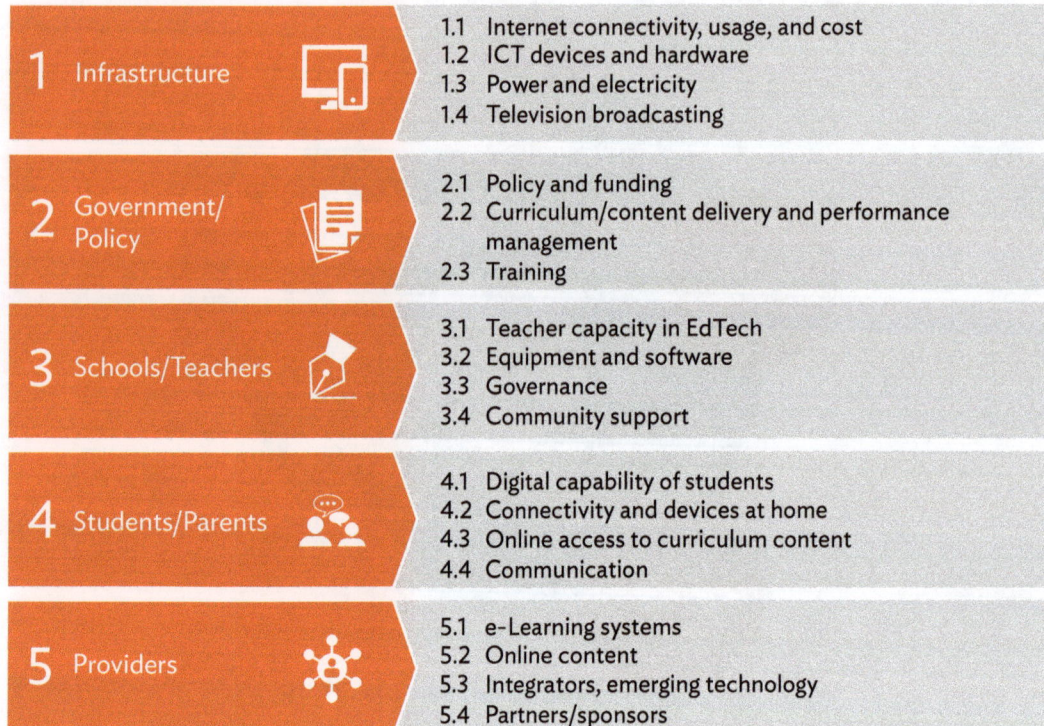

1 Infrastructure
- 1.1 Internet connectivity, usage, and cost
- 1.2 ICT devices and hardware
- 1.3 Power and electricity
- 1.4 Television broadcasting

2 Government/Policy
- 2.1 Policy and funding
- 2.2 Curriculum/content delivery and performance management
- 2.3 Training

3 Schools/Teachers
- 3.1 Teacher capacity in EdTech
- 3.2 Equipment and software
- 3.3 Governance
- 3.4 Community support

4 Students/Parents
- 4.1 Digital capability of students
- 4.2 Connectivity and devices at home
- 4.3 Online access to curriculum content
- 4.4 Communication

5 Providers
- 5.1 e-Learning systems
- 5.2 Online content
- 5.3 Integrators, emerging technology
- 5.4 Partners/sponsors

EdTech = education technology, ICT = information and communication technology.
Source: Economist Impact. 2022. *The Digital Education Readiness Framework.*

Strategy Setting

Digital transformation must be guided by a national strategy for EdTech adoption as part of education policy. Appropriate for the country's readiness stage, the strategy sets out goals, resources, core activities, key performance indicators, and timelines for the sector development.

DERF pillars can guide the structuring of a national EdTech strategy. Each pillar is equally important, and the strategy should help to rethink the system from the ground up and address every detail that enables new ways of working. Addressing all of the five pillars simultaneously is best, even if it means slower progress on a particular pillar. It makes investment more efficient and avoids having weak links that lag and hinder the use of technology.

1. **Technological infrastructure to enable digital transformation**

Providing inclusive access to physical and digital infrastructure is the foundation for a successful digital education ecosystem. UNICEF has developed the National Guide Price Generator for estimating the national costs of providing universal access to the internet and devices.[42] As the investment is substantial, it is important to formulate a strategy that ensures that it is directed toward the most pressing areas: connectivity and data affordability, access to devices, or improving the electrical grid.

The maturity of a country's technological infrastructure strongly defines how EdTech can and should be used in schools, categorized as low-, medium-, or high-tech. Figure 14 describes the main infrastructure differences.

EdTech strategy should set goals for necessary infrastructure development but also define practices that work in the current environment, be it low- or high-tech. Countries should not rush into cutting-edge EdTech activities if basic infrastructure is not yet in place.

Figure 14: Technological Infrastructure Differences

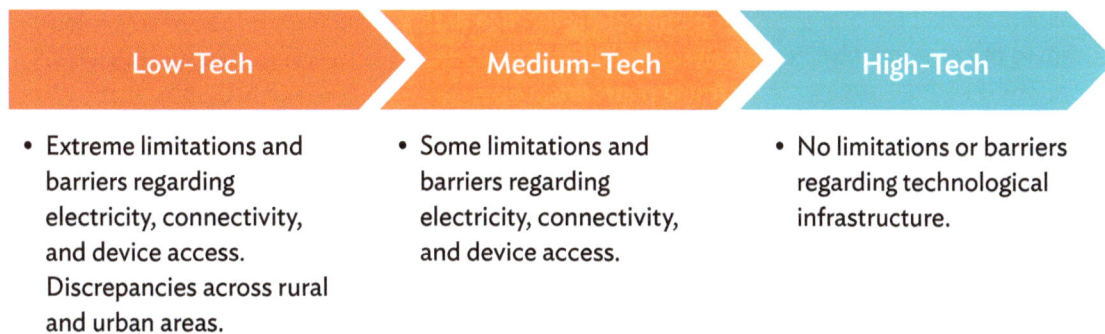

Low-Tech	Medium-Tech	High-Tech
• Extreme limitations and barriers regarding electricity, connectivity, and device access. Discrepancies across rural and urban areas.	• Some limitations and barriers regarding electricity, connectivity, and device access.	• No limitations or barriers regarding technological infrastructure.

Source: Authors.

2. **What is a favorable policy environment for the use of EdTech?**

A favorable policy environment supports long-term digital education (footnote 38). It should cover curriculum, guidelines, funding, and resource allocation, as well as standards and protocols for decision-making and responsibilities. Together with technological infrastructure, government policies create an enabling environment for teachers and students to take full advantage of technology.

Analyses of EdTech strategies in Australia, Cambodia, Finland, Malaysia, Singapore, the Republic of Korea, and the United Kingdom (UK) revealed strategic approaches to build a favorable policy environment that supports the digital transformation of education (Figure 15).

---

[42]   H. Yao et al. 2021. *How Much Does Universal Digital Learning Cost?* UNICEF.

Figure 15: Policy in Different Technological Infrastructure Environments

Low-Tech	Medium-Tech	High-Tech
• Governmentally organized pilot projects with organizations that provide funding and innovative solutions. • Centralized technology procurement, budgeting, and quality curation process. • Context-relevant guidelines and real-time support for teachers, carers, and students to use low-tech solutions in teaching learning. • Implementation of EMIS system to monitor school operations on school level. • Curriculum development to support tech-inclusive teaching learning, especially in foundational literacy and numeracy.	• School or group level pilots with partners to test innovative learning solutions and measure impact. • School or group level resource allocation and procurement with clear monitoring and guidelines. • Development of proprietary learning systems, content platforms and teacher portals that support tech-enhanced pedagogy. • Supporting data- informed decision-making through data analytics from EMIS and learning platforms. • Curriculum development to support tech-inclusive teaching and learning, focus on formative assessment and soft skills and ICT skills development.	• Schools collbborating with EdTech developers and ecosystem operators to co-develop solutions. • Creation of quality standards to guide the procurement of EdTech. • Scaling data collection and monitoring digital skill gaps nationwide with EMIS and learning systems. • Teacher education providing scientific thinking skills to enable teachers to reflect upon own use of technology. • Develop effective model for EdTech budgeting that consider infra, content, and teacher training.

EdTech = education technology, EMIS = education management information system, ICT = information and communication technology.

Source: Authors.

3.   How best to support schools' and teachers' use of EdTech

Teachers, through their own digital skills—and institutions, through their physical resources, leadership, and governance policies—are instrumental in creating a digital-friendly environment for students at all education levels (footnote 38). As teachers are the main adopters of EdTech tools, they can greatly contribute to or, alternatively, impede its use, and their performance with the tool greatly determines learning outcomes. That teachers' competence and motivation are so critical highlights the importance of leadership and support for teachers through training and adequate compensation for their active contribution in the digital transformation. Figure 16 outlines strategic approaches to support schools and teachers in the use of EdTech.

Figure 16: Support for Schools' and Teachers' Adoption of EdTech

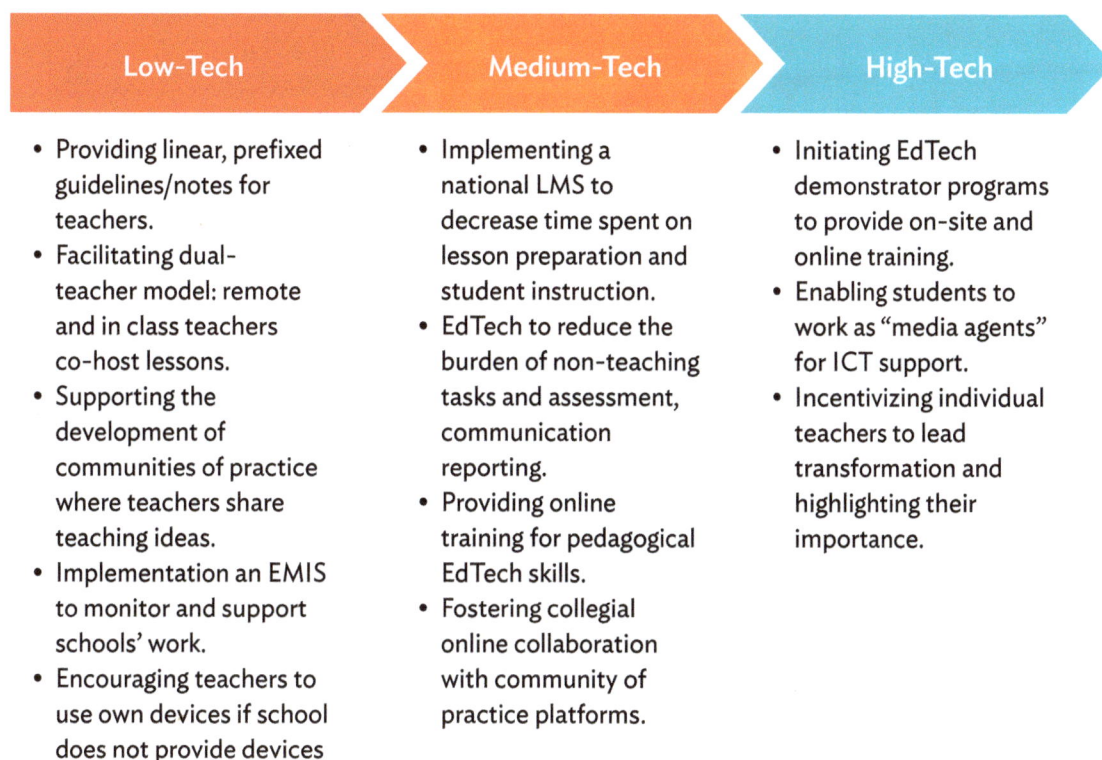

Low-Tech	Medium-Tech	High-Tech
• Providing linear, prefixed guidelines/notes for teachers. • Facilitating dual-teacher model: remote and in class teachers co-host lessons. • Supporting the development of communities of practice where teachers share teaching ideas. • Implementation an EMIS to monitor and support schools' work. • Encouraging teachers to use own devices if school does not provide devices	• Implementing a national LMS to decrease time spent on lesson preparation and student instruction. • EdTech to reduce the burden of non-teaching tasks and assessment, communication reporting. • Providing online training for pedagogical EdTech skills. • Fostering collegial online collaboration with community of practice platforms.	• Initiating EdTech demonstrator programs to provide on-site and online training. • Enabling students to work as "media agents" for ICT support. • Incentivizing individual teachers to lead transformation and highlighting their importance.

EdTech = education technology, EMIS = education management information system, ICT = information and communication technology, LMS = learning management system.
Source: Authors.

4. **How to ensure students have necessary digital capability and support at home**

The digital capability of students and their access to the tools and content required for digital education are not only key pillars of the digital education ecosystem but are also outcomes in themselves of the progress achieved across other pillars that are a part of the ADB DERF (footnote 38). As technology has become omnipresent, people need basic digital literacy that allows safe and effective interaction online. This includes the ability to self-regulate screen time and understand the importance of parental monitoring.

Supportive infrastructure and policies, and strong digital capability among teachers, together contribute to the digital readiness of students, in addition to the independent contributions of private providers and facilitative environments provided by caregivers at home. Figure 18 identifies strategic approaches through which governments can support students and parents in their use of EdTech.

Figure 17: Support for Students and Parents at Home

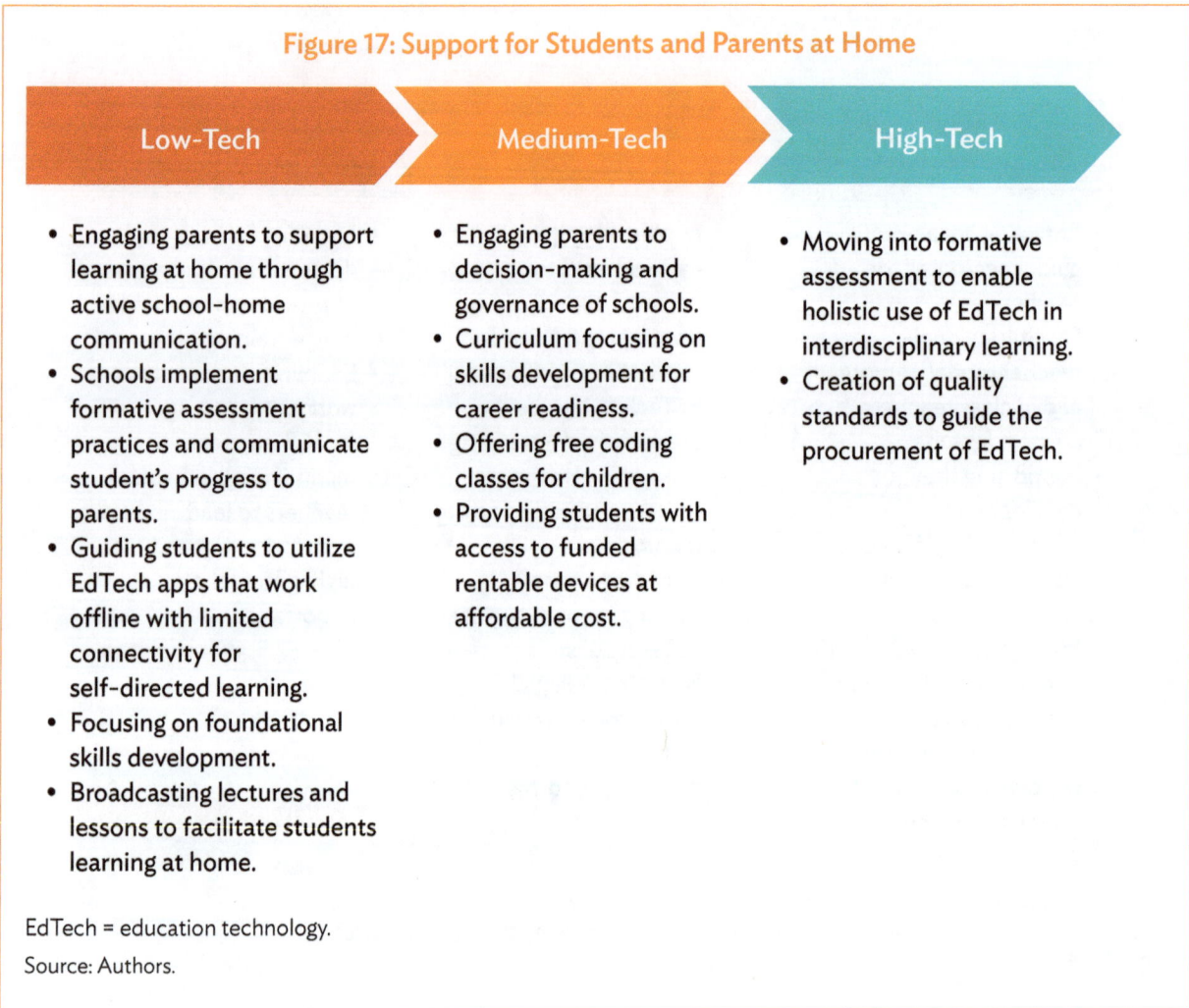

Low-Tech	Medium-Tech	High-Tech
• Engaging parents to support learning at home through active school-home communication. • Schools implement formative assessment practices and communicate student's progress to parents. • Guiding students to utilize EdTech apps that work offline with limited connectivity for self-directed learning. • Focusing on foundational skills development. • Broadcasting lectures and lessons to facilitate students learning at home.	• Engaging parents to decision-making and governance of schools. • Curriculum focusing on skills development for career readiness. • Offering free coding classes for children. • Providing students with access to funded rentable devices at affordable cost.	• Moving into formative assessment to enable holistic use of EdTech in interdisciplinary learning. • Creation of quality standards to guide the procurement of EdTech.

EdTech = education technology.
Source: Authors.

5. How to ensure the availability of high-quality EdTech solutions

The availability of high-quality products, content, and tools for learning is the fifth critical pillar in the digital education ecosystem (footnote 38). Providers of solutions can be private or public, local or international, open-source or proprietary, but the solutions need to be locally relevant and of high quality. To ensure ready availability of EdTech solutions, the country needs to create an environment in which it is worthwhile for providers to offer products and work in partnership with educational institutions to exchange knowledge.

In the longer term, developing a local ecosystem that supports EdTech can create a pool of entrepreneurs. A supportive environment would include initiatives that benefit EdTech, such as co-development with schools and export programs. Also needed is a talented workforce of developers and educational and business experts. Figure 18 identifies strategic approaches by which a government can support EdTech ecosystem development and locally attuned, high-quality EdTech tools.

Figure 18: Government Support for an EdTech Ecosystem

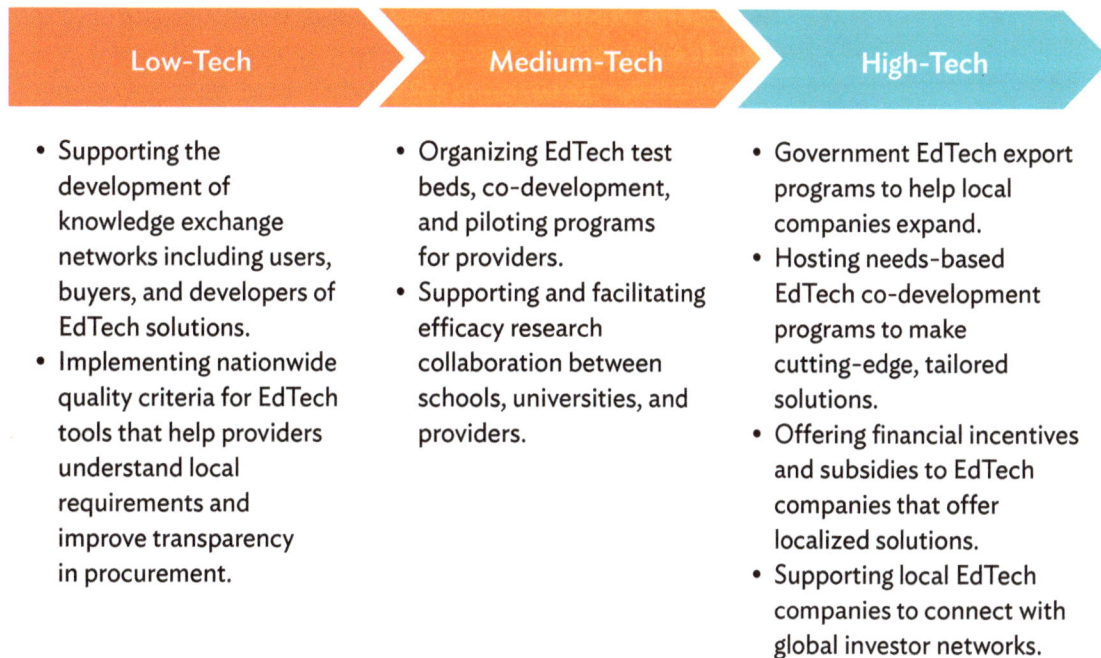

Low-Tech	Medium-Tech	High-Tech

Low-Tech

- Supporting the development of knowledge exchange networks including users, buyers, and developers of EdTech solutions.
- Implementing nationwide quality criteria for EdTech tools that help providers understand local requirements and improve transparency in procurement.

Medium-Tech

- Organizing EdTech test beds, co-development, and piloting programs for providers.
- Supporting and facilitating efficacy research collaboration between schools, universities, and providers.

High-Tech

- Government EdTech export programs to help local companies expand.
- Hosting needs-based EdTech co-development programs to make cutting-edge, tailored solutions.
- Offering financial incentives and subsidies to EdTech companies that offer localized solutions.
- Supporting local EdTech companies to connect with global investor networks.

EdTech = education technology.
Source: Authors.

EdTech product repositories of suitable solutions. As product categorization demonstrates, a vast number of opportunities exist to enhance educational practices with technology tools. However, it is not always self-evident that all existing or popular EdTech products benefit their users. Experts have expressed concern, for example, about a lack of evidence demonstrating that apps marketed as educational really have value.[43] An analysis of over 120 children's educational apps found that most did not align with learning principles and had little value. It is therefore advisable when procuring and implementing EdTech solutions to ensure their quality, effectiveness, and suitability.

Various EdTech repositories offer product options and facilitate understanding their differences. Well-known product repositories include the following:

- **EdTech Impact** is a free, comprehensive K–12 EdTech review platform that compares more than 1,500 products across 60 categories with over 10,000 up-to-date reviews. Reviews are independently submitted, published regardless of their EdTech impact scores, and cover categories such as

---

[43] M. Meyer et al. 2021. How Educational Are 'Educational' Apps for Young Children? App Store Content Analysis Using the Four Pillars of Learning Framework. *Journal of Children and Media.* 15 (4). pp. 526–548. https://doi.org/10.1080/17482798.2021.1882516.

devices and hardware, school management, pupils and parents, teachers and school leaders, and subjects.[44]

- **The EdSurge Product Index** is a community-driven database of EdTech products equipped with a search function and a short-list function for comparing products. Users can explore products by audience, product category, discipline, education level, and pricing model. The index provides validations and highlights key information across the following domains: interoperability, privacy, digital pedagogy, research evidence, usability, and accessibility. The repository currently has 694 products.[45]

- **Common Sense Education** offers 3,611 listings under its EdTech Tools section. Information is provided on how to teach with the tools, and other useful content that goes into greater detail about each tool. Users can ask the editor to review a new tool. The Common Sense program recognizes outstanding media with an official seal for quality and impact.[46]

- **Education Alliance Finland** is a Finnish vendor-facing EdTech evaluation and certification service and a repository of searchable, certified products. A wide range of EdTech products are evaluated, including e-books, apps, games, and online courses. Education Alliance Finland has a quality certification process with three areas: learning goals, pedagogical approach, and usability. Once a product has passed evaluation, it goes into the catalog and can be searched by dimension: age group, language, platform, and price.[47]

6. Effective implementation of new EdTech

Following the establishment of technological infrastructure, an EdTech-friendly operating environment, and a national strategy, digital transformation depends mainly on the effective implementation of EdTech. EdTech solutions have different end users, who have specific roles in the adoption process: teachers, students, school leaders, ICT administrators and officers, parents, and government officials. Buy-in from all these stakeholders is vital, but teachers primarily decide if and how a new tool is used in the classroom, making them the main stakeholder in EdTech adoption.

7. How to motivate teachers to use EdTech

The EdTech adoption framework describes in detail the factors that affect teachers' willingness and motivation to integrate a new EdTech tool in teaching, learning, or administration (Figure 19).

The factors cited in Figure 20 align with research findings on what affects teacher motivation. These factors should guide the work of supporting EdTech adoption at the school level but should also be addressed by education policies and guidelines. While DERF pillars support an enabling environment, the EdTech adoption

---

[44]   EdTech Impact. 2022. *EdTech Impact*. https://edtechimpact.com/.

[45]   ISTE. 2022. *EdSurge Product Index. International Society for Technology in Education*. https://index.edsurge.com/.

[46]   Common Sense Media. 2022. *Common Sense Education*. https://www.commonsense.org/education/.

[47]   Education Alliance Finland. 2022. *Education Alliance Finland. Kokoa Agency Oy*. https://www.educationalliancefinland.com.

Figure 19: EdTech Adoption Framework

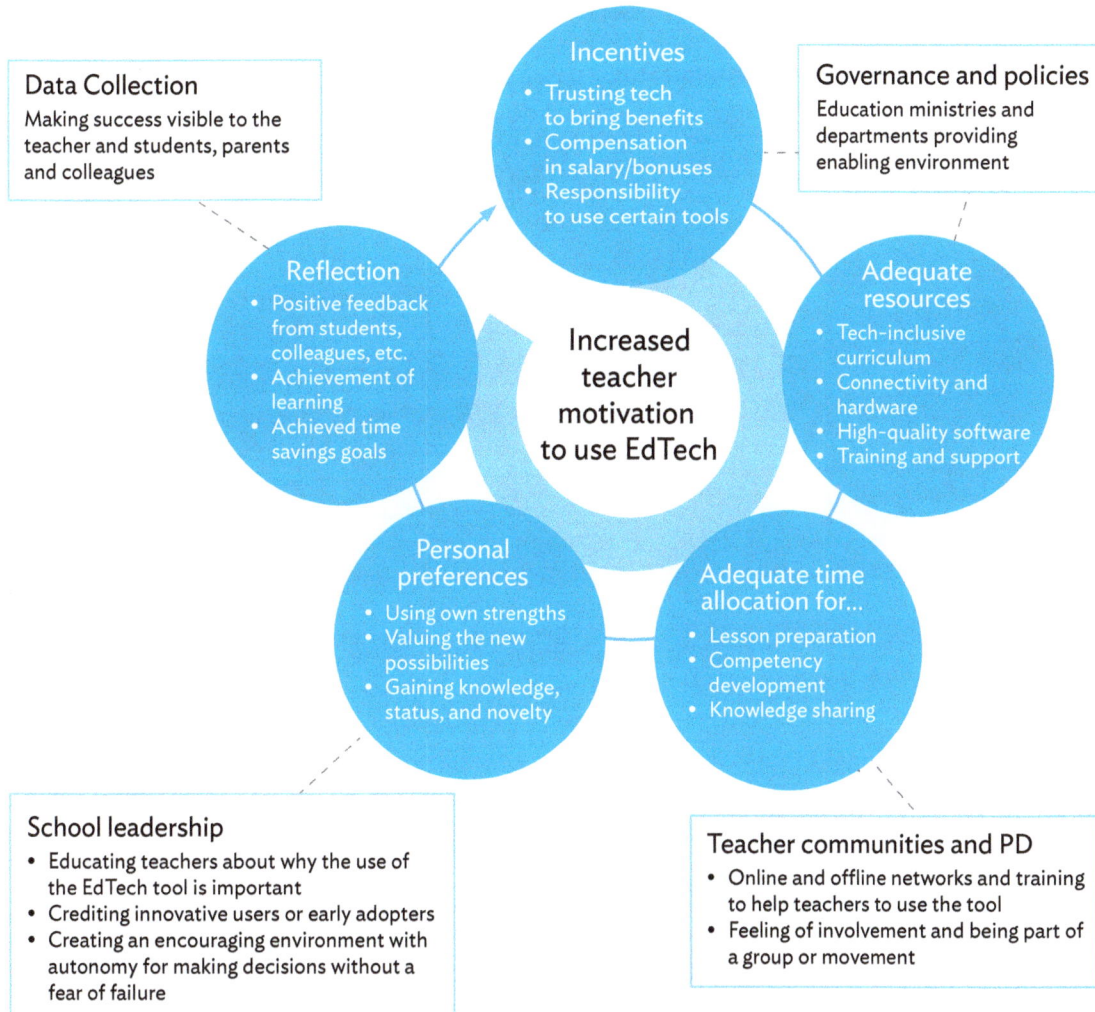

Incentives
- Trusting tech to bring benefits
- Compensation in salary/bonuses
- Responsibility to use certain tools

Data Collection
Making success visible to the teacher and students, parents and colleagues

Governance and policies
Education ministries and departments providing enabling environment

Reflection
- Positive feedback from students, colleagues, etc.
- Achievement of learning
- Achieved time savings goals

Increased teacher motivation to use EdTech

Adequate resources
- Tech-inclusive curriculum
- Connectivity and hardware
- High-quality software
- Training and support

Personal preferences
- Using own strengths
- Valuing the new possibilities
- Gaining knowledge, status, and novelty

Adequate time allocation for...
- Lesson preparation
- Competency development
- Knowledge sharing

School leadership
- Educating teachers about why the use of the EdTech tool is important
- Crediting innovative users or early adopters
- Creating an encouraging environment with autonomy for making decisions without a fear of failure

Teacher communities and PD
- Online and offline networks and training to help teachers to use the tool
- Feeling of involvement and being part of a group or movement

EdTech = education technology, PD = professional development (of teachers).
Source: Authors.

---

framework similarly highlights enabling factors but at a micro level, with most of its actions to be executed by school leaders and ICT officers.

Another description of the stages of EdTech innovation moving into teachers' daily practices is shown in Table 2. The model is a seven-stage process that describes the different concerns teachers may have as they become aware of and consider adopting an innovation.

Understanding the different stages of concerns can help the change management process and to anticipate and plan for potential challenges or roadblocks that may arise during the EdTech implementation process. By being aware of the concerns that teachers may have at different stages, it is possible to develop strategies to address those concerns and smooth the path to successful EdTech implementation.

Table 2: Description of Concerns

Stage	Name	Description of Concerns
0	Awareness	Teachers have little awareness or concern for a particular innovation. The innovation is seen not to affect them at this stage.
1	Informational	Teachers have general or vague awareness of an innovation. Teachers may begin some information seeking to gain additional knowledge about the innovation.
2	Personal	Teachers' concerns are about the personal cost of implementing an innovation—how a particular innovation will change the demands of or conflict with existing understanding of what they currently do.
3	Management	Teachers' concerns will focus around how to integrate the logistics of a particular innovation into their daily jobs.
4	Consequence	Teachers' concerns are primarily on the impact of the innovation on their students.
5	Collaboration	Teachers begin to have concerns about how they compare to their peers and how they can work with their fellow teachers on an innovation.
6	Refocusing	Teachers' concerns are how to better implement an innovation.

Source: E.T. Straub. 2009. Understanding Technology Adoption: Theory and Future Directions for Informal Learning. *Review of Educational Research.* 79 (2). pp. 625–649.

8. How to select the right EdTech tools

Success with EdTech depends on the quality and suitability of EdTech solutions. A systematic review process before procurement increases the probability that the solution is high quality; keeps users engaged; and aligns with the infrastructure, curriculum, and learning culture. A high-quality product that is fit for purpose is more likely to be used appropriately by learners, educators, parents, and other stakeholders, effectively achieving targeted results.

To support EdTech selection in terms of quality, effectiveness, scalability, affordability (QESA), ADB has developed a proprietary QESA EdTech Evaluation Framework. The QESA EdTech Evaluation Framework makes evaluation systematic and sets transparent and fair criteria for EdTech providers.

The QESA EdTech Evaluation Framework is put in practice through guiding questions. Each of the four aspects is broken down into a set of 10–20 questions, that help to pay attention to the right aspects when auditing and evaluating an EdTech solution.

Evaluating and selecting solutions should balance the four QESA elements and be appropriate for the context. Effective pedagogical design involves similar considerations in all cases, but the specific curriculum alignment, infrastructure requirements, local adaptability, and cost affordability may vary among users. In other words, the design of a teaching and learning experience should consider certain principles that apply universally, but the specifics of how these principles are implemented may differ depending on the context in which they are being used. The guiding QESA questions thus prompt the evaluator to consider the solution's suitability for a specific environment (Figure 20).

Figure 20: QESA EdTech Evaluation Framework to Guide the Selection of EdTech Solutions

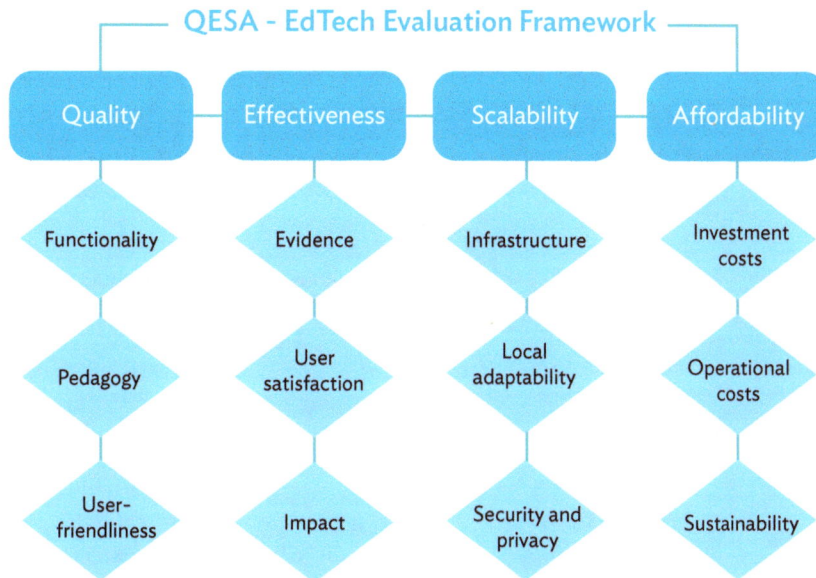

EdTech = education technology; QESA = quality, effectiveness, scalability, affordability.
Source: Authors.

The QESA EdTech Evaluation Framework focus areas are divided into subcategories, as shown in Figure 21. A link to access the full framework on Google Drive is provided below.

Appendix 2 (EdTech product evaluations using QESA) provides a sample of cases in which the QESA evaluation tool was applied to several EdTech products. It includes a table of EdTech product categories and their relevance to specific educational levels, ranging from K–12 to technical and vocational education and training and higher education. The products are also classified based on their focus, such as teaching and learning, employability and entrepreneurship, or education governance, as well as their level of technological sophistication.

Appendix 3 (QESA User Guide) and Annex 4 (QESA EdTech Evaluation Tool – Excel-based) provide guidance on how to apply the tool to evaluate an EdTech product and how to summarize the results.

9. **EdTech selection process**

The EdTech selection process can be broken down into a sequence of steps and associated tasks, with guidelines provided in the EdTech Best Practice Toolkit (Table 3).

Table 3: EdTech Selection Process and Tasks

Needs Assessment	Product and Vendor Evaluation	Sandbox Testing and In-Depth Evaluation	Request for Proposal	Contract Negotiation and Award
• Assess country's readiness for EdTech; see five pillars of digital education readiness, and DERF report • Select stakeholder group • Determine requirements using the QESA EdTech evaluation framework • Prioritize requirements using the requirement prioritization worksheet • Research product reviews on the EdTech repositories list (e.g., EdTech Hub, and Edu Impact)	• Shortlist 3–5 EdTech vendors for review based on the results from a requirements prioritization and product review • Plan use cases • Place pre-demo calls to vendors • Prepare demos using the EdTech demo guideline and checklist • Conduct demos and distribute the vendor selection score sheet to stakeholder groups	• Set up sandboxes and related materials • Heuristically evaluate using heuristic evaluation metrics • Conduct sandbox testing and reviews with each stakeholder group • Hold follow-up technical meetings with vendors • Test for bugs and troubleshoot	• Prepare and issue a request for proposal, if needed, using the template • Review and determine the top 2–3 vendors to proceed with • Check references using vendor reference check questions	• Assemble a negotiation team • Negotiate with vendors using the contract negotiation template and checklist • Validate the scope and contract award decision • Prepare for implementation

DERF = Digital Education Readiness Framework; EdTech = education technology; QESA = quality, effectiveness, scalability, and affordability.
Source: S. Lee and D. McIntosh. 2020. *LMS Selection Toolkit: A set of tools to help you choose the best LMS for your organization.* https://paradoxlearning.com/wp-content/uploads/2020/02/LMS-toolkit_Feb-2020.pdf.

> **Technology will never replace great teachers, but technology in the hands of great teachers is transformational.**
>
> **George Couros,** author of *"The Innovator's Mindset, Innovate Inside the Box, and Because of a Teacher!"*

10. **How to ensure teachers have digital and pedagogical skills to use EdTech**

Professional development in digital and pedagogical skills for using EdTech ensures that tools are used in meaningful ways. As innovations continuously change and expand, pre-service teacher education is challenged to prepare student teachers with all the competencies they need to use EdTech. This highlights the importance of in-service training and continued professional learning.

Toward understanding skill gaps on a personal or national level, a variety of tools exist to help teachers assess the digital and pedagogical competencies needed to use EdTech successfully. Some of these tools work well for self-assessment and self-improvement through reflection on one's own skills and direction for development.

Ideally, professional learning activities align with the existing skill gaps. The main supports for teachers' continuous professional learning related to EdTech utilization are massive online open courses, online programs, training offered by product vendors, and professional communities of practice. Whereas traditionally oriented training programs are useful for acquiring specific skills—for example, learning to use a certain new software—online communities can provide continuous support on demand for professional development.

11. Evaluation of digital and pedagogical competency

ADB is currently implementing a project on teachers' digital competency. The project identifies, adapts, and pilots off-the-shelf software to measure teachers' digital skills in ADB developing member countries. The Selfie for Teachers tool was selected to be piloted as part of a small-scale feasibility study in Cambodia and Uzbekistan.[48] The tool is an example of self-assessment solutions that are freely available to schools and teachers that wish to reflect upon their digital and pedagogical competency.

The Selfie for Teachers assessment includes six competency areas: professional engagement, digital resources, teachers and learning, assessment, empowering learners, and facilitating learners' digital competence (Figure 21). These areas form the structure for teacher competency in using ICT in teaching and learning in pedagogically meaningful ways.

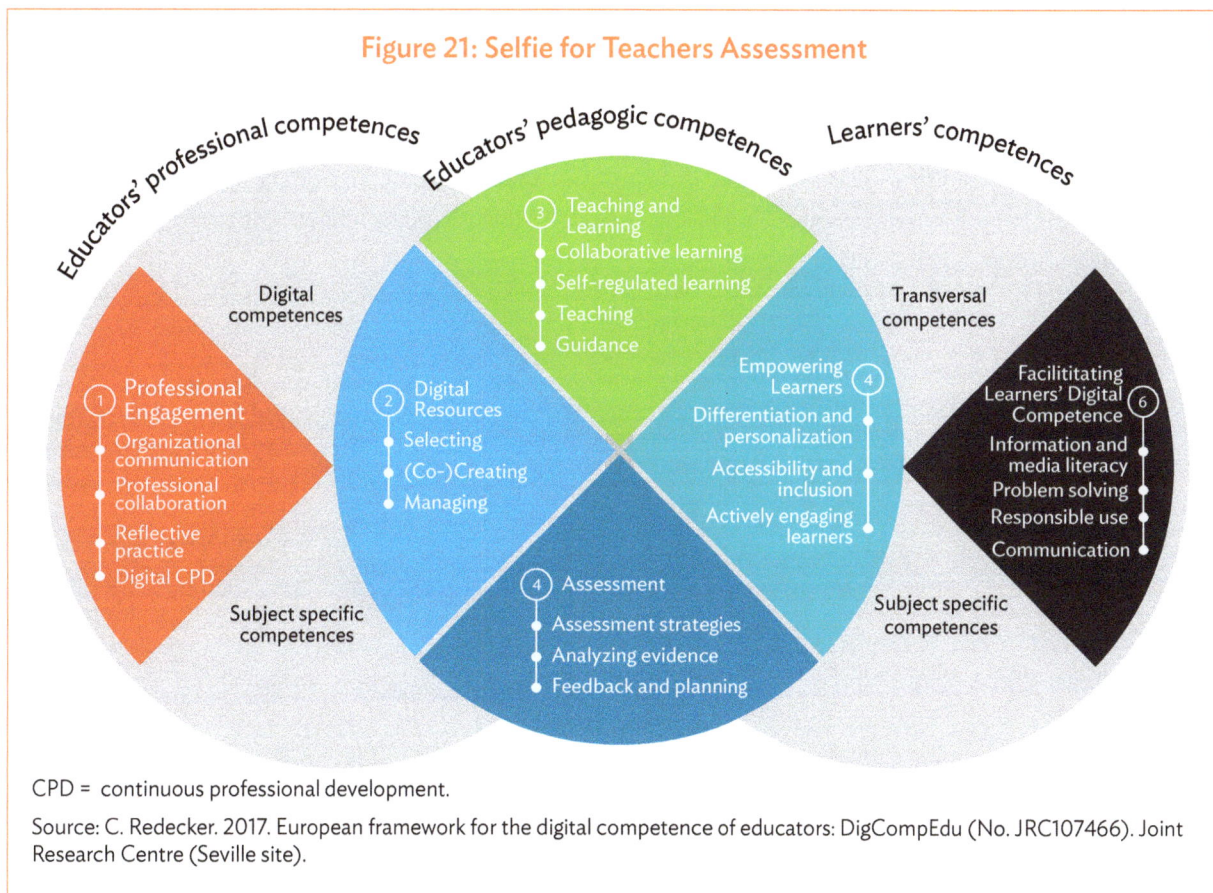

Figure 21: Selfie for Teachers Assessment

CPD = continuous professional development.

Source: C. Redecker. 2017. European framework for the digital competence of educators: DigCompEdu (No. JRC107466). Joint Research Centre (Seville site).

48   European Commission. n.d. *European Education Area: Quality Education and Training for All.* https://education.ec.europa.eu/selfie-for-teachers/how-it-works.

When school communities use this or a similar tool as part of their transformational efforts, they get a clearer picture of their teachers' readiness to use EdTech in teaching and learning. The following are assessment tools discovered and evaluated in ADB's Teacher Digital Competency Project in 2022:

(i)   UNESCO ICT Competence Framework, for Teachers
(ii) European Framework for the Digital Competence of Educators: DigCompEdu
(iii) Selfie for Teachers
(iv) Technology Enhanced Teaching Self-Assessment Tool

12. Teacher professional development through communities of practice

Informal online communities and networks are valuable sources of professional development.[49] The number of communities of practice is hence on the rise to share knowledge teacher-to-teacher. Indonesia and Bangladesh, for example, have launched national platforms for teachers to share ideas and best practices. From primary to vocational education, teachers are using the platform in Bangladesh to discuss and exchange ideas with colleagues and to store and retrieve digital education content on different subjects (Figure 22). The platform improves teachers' work in several ways, notably by making them more self-confident, efficient, and ICT-skilled, and helping them generate innovative and creative ideas through collaborative networking. Of teachers in Bangladesh, 90% have uploaded content on the platform, and 95% have downloaded content.[50]

A university in Malaysia encouraged teacher training students to use Facebook to share materials and ideas about teaching. The vast majority of participants enjoyed doing this and said that they planned to continue using it once they entered service as teachers. Students said that participating in the online community of practice made them want to be better teachers.[51]

Collegial sharing and support are also in play in the UK through an EdTech Demonstrator program.[52] The program has helped over 100,000 classroom staff implement remote learning, and it has helped 27 schools across the UK provide online training in digital pedagogies to other schools.

[49] M. Macià and I. García. 2016. Informal Online Communities and Networks as a Source of Teacher Professional Development: A Review. *Teaching and Teacher Education*. 55. pp. 291–307.
[50] H. Hansson et al. 2018. The Teachers' Portal as a Tool for Teachers' Professional Development in Bangladesh: Facilitating Nationwide Networking and Digital Multimedia Content for 40,000 Schools. *International Journal of Education and Development Using ICT*. 14 (3).
[51] N. Annamalai. 2018. Exploring the Use of Facebook and Other Social Media Sites in Pre-Service Teacher Education. *The English Teacher*. 47 (1). p. 1.
[52] Government of the United Kingdom, Department of Education. 2022. *EdTech Demonstrator Schools and Colleges: About the Programme.* https://www.gov.uk/government/publications/edtech-demonstrator-schools-and-colleges-successful-applicants/about-the-programme.

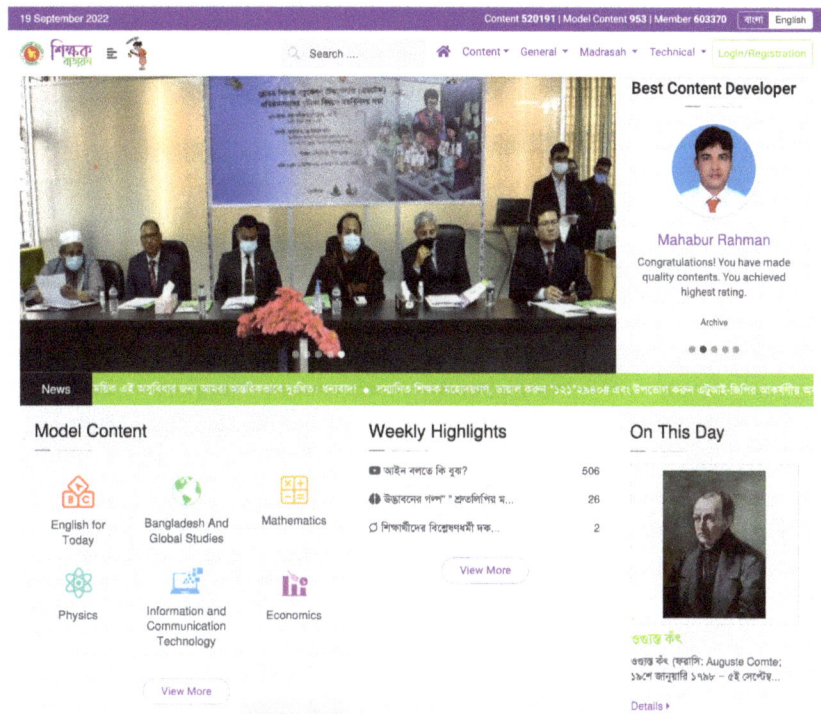

Figure 22: Screenshot from National Teachers' Platform in Bangladesh

Source: Government of Bangladesh, Ministry of Education, National Teachers' Platform. https://www.teachers.gov.bd/.

please provide the raw hires image

13. Models for the effective use of EdTech

Once EdTech adoption has advanced to a stage where teachers and students have a grip on the technology, it is time to reflect on its pedagogical use. Globally recognized frameworks for pedagogical use of technology can guide school leaders and teachers in planning and utilization.

The SAMR Model

The SAMR model (Figure 23)—the letters stand for substitution, augmentation, modifications, and redefinition—classifies the use of EdTech to work either as enhancement of current practices or as a driver of transformation. It was developed to help teachers enhance teaching, learning, and assessment and move toward using technology as an enabler of education transformation.[53]

Enhancement refers to using EdTech to supplement existing teaching and learning practices, while transformation refers to using it to redesign these practices and bring new possibilities and opportunities. These two stages can be intertwined, and the ultimate goal is often to move toward transformation. However, the success of this transition depends on the type of EdTech solution being used and the competence of the users.

---

[53]   R. Puentedura. 2010. *SAMR and TPCK: Intro to Advanced Practice.* http://hippasus.com/resources/sweden2010/SAMR_TPCK_IntroToAdvancedPractice.pdf.

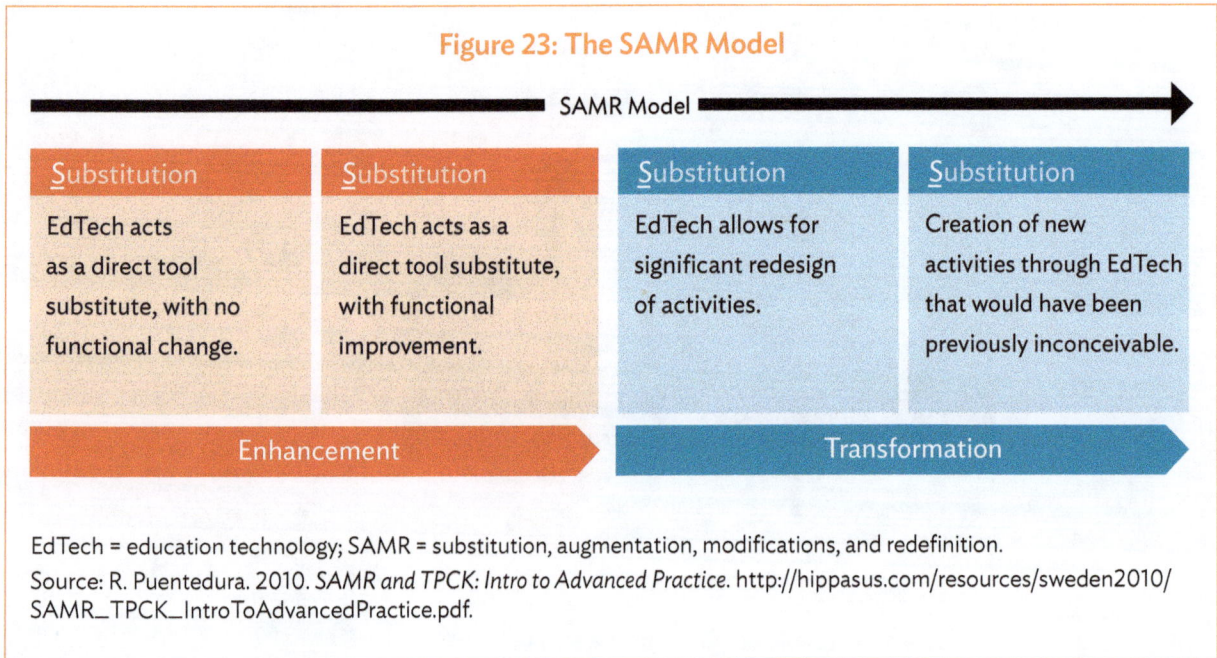

Figure 23: The SAMR Model

EdTech = education technology; SAMR = substitution, augmentation, modifications, and redefinition.
Source: R. Puentedura. 2010. *SAMR and TPCK: Intro to Advanced Practice.* http://hippasus.com/resources/sweden2010/SAMR_TPCK_IntroToAdvancedPractice.pdf.

The following examples illustrate these concepts:

- Enhancement: A teacher uses an LMS to supplement his/her traditional classroom lectures by posting notes and assignments online. The LMS enhances the teacher's existing teaching practices, but the overall structure of the class remains the same.

- Transformation: A teacher uses a virtual reality platform to completely redesign his/her lesson plan and deliver an immersive, interactive learning experience to his/her students. The platform transforms the traditional classroom lecture into a new and innovative learning experience that would not be possible without technology.

It is worth noting that not all EdTech solutions will lead to transformation. For example, using a simple calculator in a math class could be considered an enhancement, as it only supplements the teacher's existing teaching practices rather than transforming them. The type of EdTech solution and the competence of the users in using it will ultimately determine whether enhancement or transformation is achieved.

The TPACK Model

The TPACK model (Figure 24)—the letters stand for technological, pedagogical, and content knowledge—describes knowledge requirements for a teacher when using technology in education.[54] The effective implementation of EdTech requires knowledge of the subject taught, of effective pedagogies to achieve the learning goals, and of how to assess progress, as well as the technological knowledge to use the digital tools.

---

[54]   M. Koehler and P. Mishra. 2009. What Is Technological Pedagogical Content Knowledge (TPACK)? *Contemporary Issues in Technology and Teacher Education.* 9 (1). pp. 60–70.

Figure 24: The TPACK Model

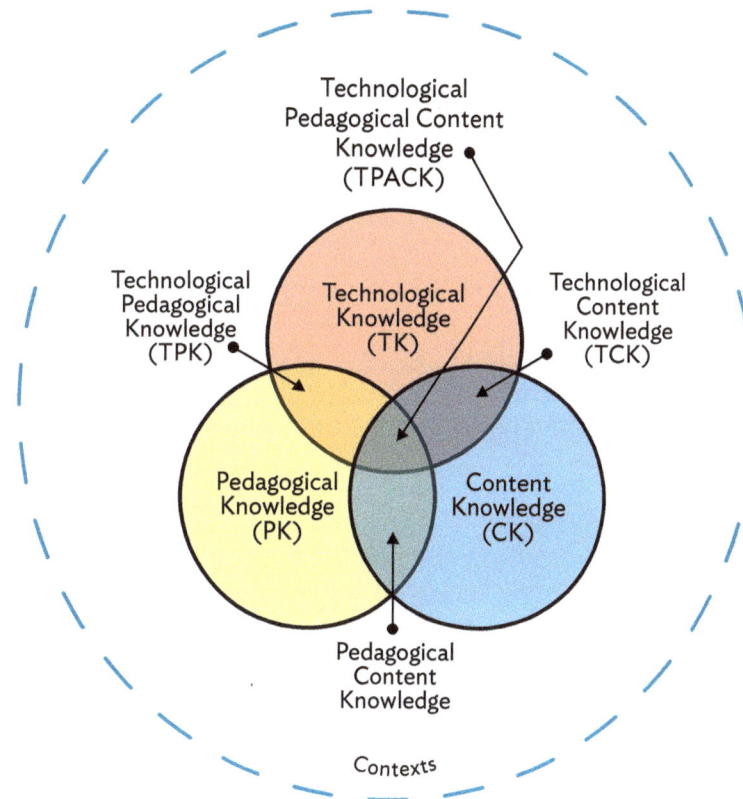

TPACK = technological, pedagogical, and content knowledge.
Source: tpack.org.

TPACK is one of the most widely cited and best recognized models to guide effective EdTech implementation. It is especially useful for mapping teachers' skill gaps and planning professional development initiatives, but it can also be used as a guide for digital learning design through its three core principles, arguing that content-driven, pedagogically valid, and technologically meaningful experiences lead to effective learning. The ways EdTech should be used in order to achieve the best results always depend on context. For example, education level, discipline, institutional culture, or users' competencies have an important influence on the choices made by a teacher.[55] The emphasis of the three knowledge areas in TPACK (content, pedagogy, and technology) varies depending on the specific context.

55   J.M. Rosenberg and M.J. Koehler. 2015. Context and Technological Pedagogical Content Knowledge (TPACK): A Systematic Review. *Journal of Research on Technology in Education.* 47 (3). pp. 186–210.

6 | Conclusions

Figure 25 presents a digital transformation road map with EdTech, including action for each transformational step. All actions should align with the country's or education system's level of digital education readiness.

Figure 25: Digital Transformation Road Map with EdTech

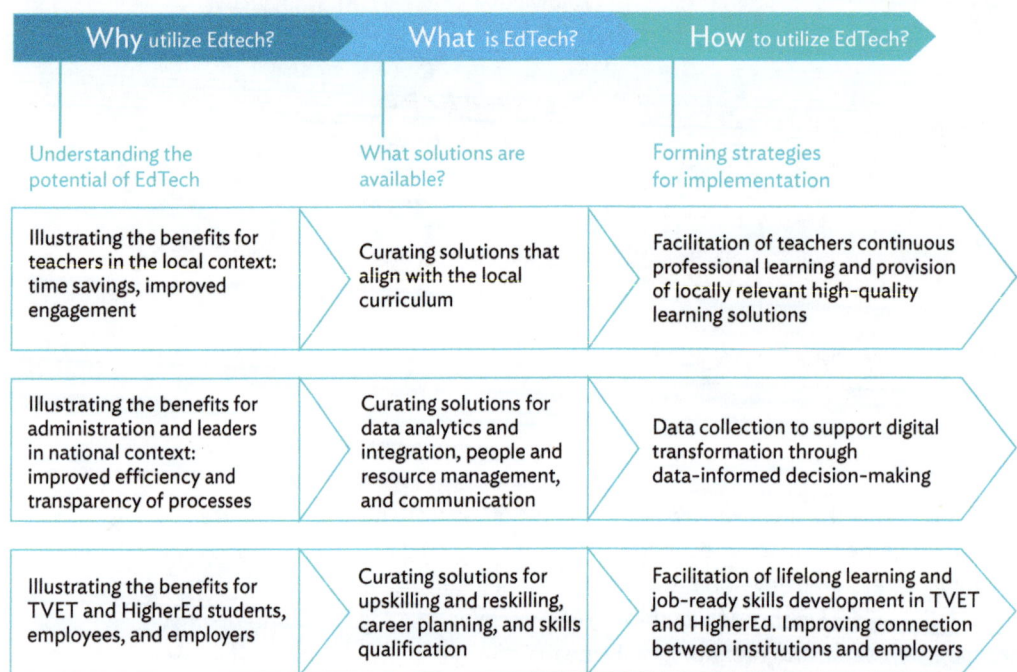

	Why utilize Edtech? Understanding the potential of EdTech	What is EdTech? What solutions are available?	How to utilize EdTech? Forming strategies for implementation
Teaching and learning	Illustrating the benefits for teachers in the local context: time savings, improved engagement	Curating solutions that align with the local curriculum	Facilitation of teachers continuous professional learning and provision of locally relevant high-quality learning solutions
Education governance	Illustrating the benefits for administration and leaders in national context: improved efficiency and transparency of processes	Curating solutions for data analytics and integration, people and resource management, and communication	Data collection to support digital transformation through data-informed decision-making
Employability and entrepreneurship	Illustrating the benefits for TVET and HigherEd students, employees, and employers	Curating solutions for upskilling and reskilling, career planning, and skills qualification	Facilitation of lifelong learning and job-ready skills development in TVET and HigherEd. Improving connection between institutions and employers

EdTech = education technology, TVET = technical and vocational education and training.
Source: Authors.

Back to basics vs. transformation as the way forward. Virtual reality is at its best as an immersive experience in which your senses are heightened. That is an example of how modern technology can improve learning, but how EdTech is used is much more important than the technology itself. Success is achieved, not by the device or the software, but how they are used.

Advanced technologies, such as AI and augmented reality/virtual reality, are likely to catalyze a shift from traditional teacher-centric models to digital age learner-centered learning. In this new paradigm, teachers may transition from being "sages on the stage" to facilitators, coaches, and mentors. These technologies could empower personalized adaptive learning, by enhancing student engagement and providing instant individualized feedback. As a result, the education landscape might transform to prioritize student needs, promoting lifelong learning, and expanding educational opportunities across the globe. The effective use of virtual reality and the transformational power of EdTech do not happen by just equipping a classroom with headsets, nor do they happen through proficiency with technology. Reimagining tech-inclusive education requires long-term development through a systematic approach, starting with the foundational aspects necessary for an enabling environment: policies and funding, electricity, hardware and devices, connectivity, and affordable EdTech solutions. In an enabled environment, educators who are trained to use EdTech can facilitate pedagogically meaningful use of the technology. Achieving this vision requires intentional decision-making and preparation at the national and local levels. It requires going back to basics to ensure that students acquire basic literacy and numeracy, as well as the necessary digital skills.

When the enabling environment and basics align for the use of EdTech, digitization of education processes can be effectively scaled up, and that is when transformation truly starts.

Illustrative Cases of Integration of Technology in Education

Education Level	EdTech product categories	Tech Level of Application	Cases
Preschool	Teaching and Learning	Low	Case 1 (BRAC): Play-based early childhood development programs.
K–12	Teaching and Learning	Low/ Medium	Case 2 (Bridge International Academies): Technology-enabled quality education in underserved communities.
			Case 3 The Learning Equality: Deploying online learning to offline communities.
			Case 4 Tangerine: Transforming educational assessments with Tangerine mobile learning assessment app.
		Medium/ High	Case 5 BYJU: Personalized learning to close the achievement gap.
			Case 6 Enuma: Empowering independent personalized learning through inclusive and accessible EdTech solutions for children.
			Case 7 Akadasia: a global community of educators providing 21st Century education to educators and providing access to better income opportunities.
		High	Case 8 MathCloud: Adaptive learning to improve student math competencies and quality of teaching.
			Case 9 Edulastic: Closing Skill Gaps with Personalized Assessments.
TVET	Employability and entrepreneurship	Medium/ High	Case 10 TESDA Online Program: TVET for global competitiveness and work readiness.
Higher Education	Teaching and Learning	Low/ Medium	Case 11 PhET Simulations: Revolutionizing Global STEM Education for All.
		High	Case 12 Minerva: Reshaping higher education for the 21st century.
			Case 13 Udacity: Building advanced skills and credentials through nanodegrees.
	Employability and Entrepreneurship	High	Case 14 JobTech: powering career pathways with data science and AI.

continued on next page

Table *continued*

Education Level	EdTech product categories	Tech Level of Application	Cases
Reskill & Lifelong	Employability an Entrepreneurship	Medium/ High	Case 15 Gnowbe: mobile-first and learning on the go
			Case 16 Singapore skills-future program: upskilling and reskilling online courses for adult workers
		High	Case 17 Udemy: online marketplace for life-long learning and professional development
All levels	Teaching and Learning	Medium/ High	Case 18 Double Teacher: Transforming Rural Education in China through EdTech and Collaborative Learning
	Education Governance	Medium	Case 19 Learning Possibility: tools and platform supporting school data management and teaching and learning
			Case 20 OpenEMIS: education management system helping monitor and manage education systems, by offering various information management tools

Case Study 1 (Preschool)—BRAC's Play Labs and Remote Play-based learning program

Play-based early childhood development programs

BRAC, a global development organization, has been a pioneer in implementing innovative, scalable, and cost-effective educational solutions, particularly for underprivileged communities. Among their initiatives, BRAC's Play Labs and Remote Play-Based Learning Program focus on fostering early childhood development and quality education through play-based learning methodologies.

BRAC Play Labs are community-based early learning centers designed for children aged 3 to 5. They provide a safe, nurturing, and stimulating environment where children can learn through play, develop social and emotional skills, and build a strong foundation for lifelong learning.

The key features of BRAC Play Labs include play-based curriculum include a **child-centered, play-based curriculum** that promotes holistic development and learning across cognitive, social, emotional, and physical domains. The Play Labs are run by local community members, known as Play Leaders, who receive training and support from BRAC to implement the play-based curriculum and foster a positive learning environment. BRAC involves parents and community members in the Play Labs, encouraging their participation in children's learning and ensuring a sense of ownership and sustainability. BRAC Play Labs have been successfully scaled across several countries, reaching thousands of children and demonstrating a cost-effective model for early childhood education.

In response to the COVID-19 pandemic and the closure of educational institutions, BRAC adapted its **Play Lab model for remote learning, providing quality early learning opportunities for children aged 3–5 in low-resource settings**.[1] In Bangladesh, BRAC branded it "Pashe Achhi", a Remote Play-Based Learning Program, **leveraging technology and community networks to support children's learning and development**. The model reaches over 37,000 caregivers, over 100,000 children, and their families every week through 1,106 trained front liners while **Radio Play Labs reach millions of additional children with play-based learning content through local radio stations**. This has allowed BRAC to reach over 80% of children in camps and more than 90% of beneficiaries in host communities.

The key features of the program include **remote learning materials such as pre-recorded lessons, activity sheets, and storybooks, to support children's learning at home while maintaining a focus on play-based methodologies**. Play Leaders and community volunteers maintain regular contact with families, providing guidance on using remote learning materials and offering support for children's learning and well-being. The program encourages parents to play an active role in their children's learning by providing them with resources, guidance, and support to facilitate play-based activities at home.

In 2022, **UNESCO published a case study** on "Evidence and Learning: Strengthening crisis and risk-related data and institutional education information system" on BRAC's programs.[2]

Case Study 2 (K–12)—Bridge International Academies

Academy in a Box: Technology-enabled quality education in underserved communities

"Academy in a Box" model brings technology in low infrastructure environments. Providing quality and affordable education to children is a challenge particularly in underserved, low-income communities. To achieve this, Bridge International Academies leveraged technology to improve teaching and learning where power supply is intermittent and network connectivity is poor. Thus far, Bridge has reached more than 100,000 students and employed 8,000 teachers in over 450 nursery and primary schools.

---

[1]   Yidan Prize, Play-based early childhood development programs. https://yidanprize.org/education-initiatives/overview/brac/.

[2]   United Nations Education, Scientific and Cultural Organization (UNESCO). 2022. Case Study – BRAC Institute of Educational Development. https://inee.org/sites/default/files/resources/Case%20Study%20-%20BRAC_Pashe_Achhi_2022-BAT.pdf.

Delivery of quality education through wireless technology platform combined with the use of Wi-Fi-enabled smartphones. The technology-enabled learning ecosystem includes a robust, standardized curriculum developed by education experts . Teacher guides and lesson scripts are digitally published to a tablet. These are linked to the Bridge central data system allowing real-time monitoring of student progress, tracking assessment scores and the teacher performance in instructional delivery and classroom management. Having ready-made Bridge lesson scripts reduce the burden of routine tasks for teachers allowing them to spend more time on individual student needs. Training of teachers is provided regularly to update their teaching skills using the latest pedagogy.

Bridge students learned twice as much in reading and more than twice as much in math. In 2013, the Early Grade Reading Assessment and Early Grade Math Assessment results showed that 30% and 31% of Bridge pupils passed the fluent and emergent benchmarks for reading respectively, compared to 16% and 24% of pupils in neighboring schools.[3] These outcomes in reading fluency and comprehension indicate that students learn an additional 16 words per minute and gain 252 additional learning days. Bridge students also have higher school acceptance rates to national secondary schools (65% higher chance) with over 100 students receiving full four-year scholarships for secondary school.[4] In India, Bridge students also demonstrated significant improvements in reading and math compared to their non-Bridge peers.[5]

Case Study 3 (K–12)—The Learning Equality

Deploying online learning to offline communities

As of November 2021, an estimated 2.9 billion people had no access to the internet.[6] This also means no access to learning opportunities nor access to the benefits of a thriving digital economy. The Learning Equality, created in 2012 as a social impact initiative, committed to digitally bridge the gap in education by providing open educational resources around the globe through low-bandwidth and offline channels.[7]

An open-source platform provides low-resource communities with offline access to learning content. Learning Equality created KA Lite, an open-source platform which allows offline access to Khan Academy's 9,000 videos and exercises. It is customizable for personal, classroom, or school use and includes such features as performance tracking, instant feedback, gamification, and coach dashboards.

---

3   https://www.bridgeinternationalacademies.com/impact/kenya/.
4   https://www.ifc.org/wps/wcm/connect/ae0efffa-20c6-416d-98b5-8c3bce48cdff/Bridge_FINAL_low+res.pdf?MOD=AJPERES.
5   Bridge International Academies: Empowering Governments to Transform Education Quality at Statewide Scale.
6   https://www.itu.int/hub/2021/11/facts-and-figures-2021-2-9-billion-people-still-offline/#:~:text=An%20estimated%2037%20per%20cent,still%20never%20used%20the%20Internet.
7   https://www.vodafone.com/content/dam/vodafone/connectededucation/vodafone_connected_education.pdf.

Its portability allows for its use anywhere, with a variety of access options such as connecting the KA Lite to a local server where students and their devices are connected, or directly connecting the KA Lite to a student's device.

A subsequent technology innovation, Kolibri, provides expanded features to allow seamless authoring, and peer-to-peer sharing. Kolibri's content library includes subject-specific videos, reading materials, simulations, and games; literacy-building libraries of children's books; life skills materials on subjects such as health, safety, trauma recovery and digital literacy. Locally relevant content can be developed through customization features and interactivity is enhanced through instant feedback. Teachers can provide personalized recommendations, and mentor-peer blended learning context. Teachers also benefit from using pedagogical tools to aid in classroom instruction, access to lesson plans, content refreshers, pedagogical guides, and classroom management resources.

Responding to COVID-19, Learning Equality published the resources in an "At-Home section" of the Kolibri EdTech Toolkit to guide parents, educators, and learners considering the shift to distance learning during the pandemic. Content Library in Kolibri is also expanded by including COVID-19-specific resources and knowledge. Learning Equality also provides the support for implementing organizations on setting up servers, provisioning devices, and supporting hardware distribution programs to make organized content widely available.[8]

Learning Equality has over 4.3 million learners in 175 countries with little to no access to the internet. Through content partners (Khan Academy, TESS, PhET Interactive simulations), hardware partners (Google, SanDisk), and implementation partners (UNCHR, UNICEF, FUNSEPA), Learning Equality has expanded its reach and impact. KA Lite and Kolibri has also been shared in areas of more dire need such as prisons, orphanages, community centers and refugee camps.

Evaluation studies revealed positive outcomes in student learning in low-resource communities where Learning Equality's technology was used. In Guatemala, an independent evaluation found that student math performance using Khan academy content increased an average increase of 10 points in math scores compare to the traditional program.[9] In Cameroon, math skills of students improved resulting in a score increase of 13.8 points over the past performance.

---

8   https://docs.google.com/document/d/1rAsGo2z-agLLxi0DPg_qLPWHMhUWQgUGN9TzzD0W36U/edit.
9   https://learningequality.org/media/FUNSEPA_Final_Evaluation_Report_27May2016.pdf.

Case Study 4 (K-12)—Tangerine

Transforming educational assessments with Tangerine mobile learning assessment app.

Tangerine is an innovative mobile learning assessment tool developed by RTI International that aims to transform educational assessments by making them more accessible, efficient, and affordable. The tool enables educators and administrators to collect data using tablets, eliminating the need for cumbersome and error-prone paper-based assessments. By digitalizing the process, Tangerine reduces data entry errors and accelerates the analysis and reporting of results.

To date, **Tangerine has been used in over 60 countries, with the support of donors such as United States Agency for International Development (USAID), the World Bank, and the Bill & Melinda Gates Foundation.** The tool has facilitated the collection of **more than 1.5 million assessment**s, leading to more informed decision-making in education policy and practice. The impact of Tangerine has been significant, enabling organizations to track student progress, evaluate the effectiveness of interventions, and ultimately, improve learning outcomes for millions of students around the world.

Tangerine's **offline capabilities ensure that it is suitable for use in remote and low-resource settings** where internet connectivity is unreliable. Once a connection is re-established, the data can be easily synchronized with a central server, allowing for real-time monitoring and reporting.

The software has a user-friendly interface, making it easy for even first-time users to create and administer assessments. Tangerine is customizable and versatile, allowing users to adapt assessments to different curricula, languages, and grade levels.[10] It can also be used for various purposes, such as early grade reading and mathematics assessments, classroom observations, and teacher professional development evaluations.

In Kenya, Tangerine was utilized as a part of the Tusome Early Grade Reading Activity program, supported by USAID and the Kenyan Ministry of Education.[11] The platform enabled teachers and head teachers to conduct formative assessments, track student progress, and provide targeted feedback. As a result, the program achieved significant improvements in student reading outcomes and overall learning achievements.

In Tanzania, Tangerine was used for the Early Grade Reading Assessment, funded by the World Bank and the Global Partnership for Education. The tool allowed teachers to collect and analyze assessment data in real-time, enabling them to make data-driven decisions to support student learning. The results showed substantial improvements in student reading comprehension, fluency, and literacy skills.

---

[10]   DigitalPrinciples.org. 2022. *Tangerine: Mobile Assessments Made Easy*. https://digitalprinciples.org/resource/tangerine-mobile-assessments-made-easy/.

[11]   https://documents1.worldbank.org/curated/en/434231631131238626/pdf/Coach-Spotlight-Tusome-Early-Grade-Reading-Activity-EGRA.pdf.

The Tangerine assessment tool was also used in an early grade reading program in Nepal, supported by the Global Partnership for Education and UNICEF.[12] The platform facilitated easy data collection and analysis, allowing teachers to identify learning gaps and provide targeted support. Consequently, the program led to notable improvements in student reading outcomes and overall learning achievements.

In conclusion, the case studies highlighted in this summary demonstrate the effectiveness of Tangerine mobile learning assessment tool in improving early grade reading and student learning outcomes. The platform's digital assessment capabilities, real-time data analysis, and ease of use have played a crucial role in the success of various educational programs across different countries. As a result, Tangerine has become an invaluable tool for educators, administrators, and organizations working toward enhancing student learning experiences and outcomes.

Case Study 5 (Grades 4-12)—BYJU's Future School

Personalized learning to close the achievement gap

In India, school attendance is high but children are not learning basic literacy and numeracy. For example, 50% of 5th graders do not have the reading skills expected of a second grader; 75% of 3rd grade students cannot perform two-digit subtraction. In 2009, India ranked among the lowest (74 out of 75) in the global Program for International Assessment.

To increase student motivation and break the cycle of rote learning, BYJU's developed a personalized learning app and online tutoring programs for K–12 students. Studies show that students achieve greater academic progress in schools using personalized learning strategies. BYJU's The Learning App combines content, technology and media to fully deliver its lessons (Figure 29). An estimated 16 million students are learning from BYJU's app.[13]

To verify content quality, experts in their respective fields collaborated to structure the pedagogy of each subject. Gamified content is used to promote student engagement and encourage increased hours of learning. For Grades 4–10, the content is focused on conceptual learning. For Grades 11–12, the goal is to prepare students for competitive exams. A standard 100 hours of content per subject is available to ensure mastery of the learning content. After each lesson, users are quizzed to ascertain learning level. The algorithm tracks the student's understanding of the lessons and allows the student to revisit the material. The key features of the app, include:

---

[12]   https://www.globalreadingnetwork.net/sites/default/files/eddata/Using_Mobile_Technology_to_Improve_Early_Grade_Reading_Tangerine.pdf.

[13]   Mobile app download link (for Android). https://play.google.com/store/apps/details?id=com.byjus.thelearningapp&hl=en.

- engaging video lessons help students visualize concepts and understand the solutions;
- personalized learning journeys adapts to each student's pace, progress, strengths and weaknesses;
- mapped syllabus with related concepts; and
- unlimited practice to help each student master the concepts and the learning material.

Nine out of 10 parents surveyed reported an improvement in their child's grades. The ultimate measure of BYJU's technology is the impact on student learning outcomes. Increased student engagement has also encouraged greater student efforts that leads to more hours of learning using the app. BYJU's has received several awards in recognition of its effectiveness as a learning app and attracted several key investors including the Chan-Zuckerberg Initiative and the International Finance Corporation.[14]

Case Study 6 (Grades 0–12)—Enuma

Empowering Independent Learning: Inclusive and Accessible EdTech Solutions for Children

Enuma is an EdTech company specializing in designing accessible and engaging learning solutions for children with special needs, specifically focusing on early literacy and numeracy skills. Enuma's core products include Kitkit School, Todo Math, and Todo English.

Kitkit School is an award-winning tablet-based learning program designed for children aged 4–6. With a comprehensive curriculum covering literacy and math skills, the app's personalized learning experience adapts to each child's needs, fostering independent learning. **Kitkit School's impact is significant, having reached over 1.7 million children across 50+ countries worldwide.** Their learning solution has shown an average 45% improvement in math scores and a 29% improvement in literacy scores. Kitkit School has garnered several awards, including the Global Learning XPRIZE, which recognizes innovative educational solutions.[15]

Todo Math is a daily practice app that helps preschool to 2nd-grade students build essential math skills. Featuring engaging activities and games, Todo Math is designed to accommodate diverse learning styles and abilities, including students with learning disabilities. The app provides scaffolded support and adjusts to each student's progress, making math accessible and enjoyable for all children.

---

[14]   International Finance Corporation. 2018. BYJU'S: How a Learning App is Promoting Deep Conceptual Understanding that is Improving Educational Outcomes in India. *Cultivating a Love of Learning in K–12* . International Finance Corporation.

[15]   XPRIZE: https://www.xprize.org/prizes/global-learning/teams/kitkit_school.

Todo English is an innovative English language learning app designed by Enuma for children aged 6–11. The app focuses on improving listening, speaking, reading, and writing skills while following a leveled curriculum aligned with CEFR and Cambridge English standards. Todo English offers over 200 lessons, interactive games, and stories that are adaptable to various learning environments. The app's self-paced, engaging content provides children with an enjoyable learning experience, while its real-time feedback and rewards motivate students to progress. Todo English aims to empower children worldwide by offering them a comprehensive English language education.

All Children Reading is an initiative in partnership with the United States Agency for International Development (USAID), World Vision, and the Australian Government. The project aims to improve reading outcomes for children in low-resource environments. Enuma contributes to this goal by offering their technology and expertise in creating accessible and engaging learning solutions.

Enuma's impact has been recognized globally,[16] as they have partnered with governments, NGOs, and international organizations to implement their learning solutions for children, particularly in low-resource settings. Their solutions have been deployed in various regions, including Asia, Africa, and the Middle East, reaching millions of children worldwide.

Case Study 7 (K–12 and beyond)—Akadasia

A global community of educators providing 21st Century education to educators and providing access to better income opportunities.

Akadasia, founded in 2020, provides a digital learning platform for educators and educational institutions across the Asia-Pacific region. Headquartered in Singapore, it has regional operations across six countries that support over 200,000 teachers from 35 countries. Their platform offers various solutions to educational institutions, such as professional development, curriculum management, and support tools for administrators. With a **strong focus on bridging the gap between traditional and digital learning experiences**, Akadasia aims to **promote innovative teaching practices and 21st century skills**. Through its innovative products and services, such as CollabED, SkillED, and designED, Akadasia aims to empower educators and learners worldwide.

CollabED is a holistic education management system designed to streamline the learning process by providing an integrated platform that connects students, teachers, and parents. This platform enables efficient communication, planning, and monitoring of student progress. Key features include **attendance management,**

---

[16]   EdSurge. 2018. How Enuma's Games Help Kids Around the World Learn. https://www.edsurge.com/news/2018-08-21-how-enuma-s-games-help-kids-around-the-world-learn.

personalized learning plans, digital lesson planning, and real-time analytics that facilitate data-driven decision-making.

SkillED is a competency-based learning platform that focuses on enhancing student engagement and mastery of essential skills. The platform utilizes interactive, game-based learning modules to motivate students and create personalized learning experiences. With a curriculum-aligned and skills-centric approach, SkillED supports self-paced learning and encourages learners to take control of their educational journey.

designED is Akadasia's creative hub, providing instructional design services and custom eLearning solutions tailored to meet the unique needs of schools, institutions, and organizations. By offering **bespoke content development, designED helps educational institutions create engaging, immersive learning experiences** that promote better understanding and retention of knowledge.

In late 2022, Akadasia has announced a content development partnership with India's leading teacher training experts OrangeSlates. As part of the partnership, **OrangeSlates will offer its teacher upskilling and reskilling content to teachers from all over Asia and will make use of Akadasia's blockchain-based digital credentialing technology to certify and issue tamper-proof and verifiable digital credentials to teachers** who complete their courses through the Akadasia platform.[17]

In addition to these key offerings, Akadasia's extensive partner network[18] allows the company to deliver end-to-end education solutions, ranging from curriculum development to assessment and training. This collaborative approach ensures that educational institutions and learners benefit from the latest advances in education technology, thus enabling them to thrive in today's ever-evolving digital landscape.

Case Study 8 (Secondary)—MathCloud

Adaptive learning to improve student math competencies and quality of teaching

Many students struggle with math, a common challenge across countries at various grade levels and ages.[19] Some students learn faster than others, yet everyone is taught at the same pace since there is only one teacher in a standard classroom. Learning materials are not context-appropriate and fail to address the student's individual

---

[17] EdTechReview (India). https://www.edtechreview.in/news/singapores-akadasia-signs-content-development-partnership-with-indias-teacher-training-experts-orangeslates/.

[18] Singapore's Akadasia Signs Content Development Partnership with India's Teacher Training Experts OrangeSlates. https://www.edtechreview.in/.

[19] M. Haghverdi. 2012. *Recognition of Students' Difficulties in Solving Mathematical Word Problems from the Viewpoint of Teachers.*

learning needs. Memorization of solutions, rather than critical thinking skills, becomes the student's learning strategy in taking exams.

MathCloud provides a responsive learning platform to track student progress and recommend individualized learning path. Developed as a neural adaptive learning program, the technology solution defines a learning process based on an understanding of how the brain recognizes and processes information (Figure 30). Recognizing that individualized learning is key to help students learn and understand math, the unique components of the program include: (I) Question Type Hyperspace which stores problem histories of the students in classifications of problems, difficulties and category; Artificial Neural Network model algorithm which extracts problems to help create the individualized experience for the student; with the assessment how well student performs within particular math concept learning modules, a Neural Network Engine which detects weakness, predicts performance and recommends strategy to focus on problem areas; and a Personalized Encyclopedia which allows the visualization of the student's rate of understanding and displays this understanding in layers of concepts, including K–12 math concepts.

ADB's pilot tests in Sri Lanka and Bhutan using MathCloud showed positive impacts in learning outcomes. In Sri Lanka, student achievement improved by 0.4 standard deviations (7% of the highest possible score), increased students' standardized score 0.11 to 0.25 standard deviations above the mean, and the largest impact was for the subsample of students that had a common mathematics teacher across treatment and control groups, underscoring the importance of teacher and teaching quality for better results; and Khan Academy video tutorials increased students' standardized test scores by 0.21 standard deviations above the mean. In Bhutan, MathCloud improved students' raw test scores by around 10% of the highest possible score.[20] Teacher support was critical in achieving quality learning outcomes. The program helped them to identify the learning gaps and focus on coaching weaker students.

---

[20]   ADB. 2018. *Completion Report. Learning from e-learning: Testing Intelligent Learning Systems in South Asian Countries*. Manila.

Case Study 9 (K–12)—Edulastic

Closing Skill Gaps with Personalized Assessments: Edulastic's Innovative Approach to Enhancing Learning and Mastery

In a typical class, no student is typical. In any 5th grade math class, students' actual learning level may range from 3rd grade to 8th grade. To help all students master the required grade-level skills, each teacher must continually assess each student and provide differentiated instruction to fill skill gaps.

Edulastic, a cloud- and browser-based app for personalized assessment, provides teachers and students an easy way to identify skill gaps and track progress toward skills mastery. Teachers can easily create assessments for any skill using Edulastic's 30+ expert-created interactive question types and by choosing questions from more than 20,000 high-quality open-source items. Questions can include multimedia such as embedded video, audio, images, complex mathematical symbols and multi-language characters. As students complete assessments, teachers get instant data on student understanding by skill, so they can adjust instruction in real-time. Instant feedback provided to students supports skill mastery, as they can review and correct misunderstandings while their minds are still engaged with the concept.

Responding to COVID-19, Edulastic provides dozens of tools to assist teachers to teach from home effectively, like integration with Google video class and real-time student engagement data. Teachers are also able to obtain additional distance learning resources and utilize Edulastic to develop engaging eLearning lessons.

Edulastic works on nearly any Internet-connected device, mini-tablet or larger, and includes paper-based assessment options that can be auto-scored using a smartphone. It serves all levels, from early primary school to college and university courses, in multiple subjects and many languages.

More than 400,000 teachers and 10 million students use Edulastic to gauge student learning and effectively differentiate their instruction. More than 3,000 of these teachers log in from outside the United States, including dozens of Asian countries using the instant data teacher dashboard. Edulastic and the data it provides played a critical role in improving skill mastery in **Paragould School District**, which serves about 3,000 students in a high-poverty area in rural Arkansas. In 2017, the district implemented custom Edulastic assessments to identify each student's individual skill gaps. Then they focused everyone in the institution on filling those gaps and getting the students to 75% standards mastery.

"When we got our test scores back at the end of the year, we were really excited about the growth we had within our school district," says Matt McGowan, Technology Integration and Math Specialist at Paragould School District. For growth in the state of Arkansas, Paragould Junior High School was number one in mathematics and Oak Grove Middle School was number three in literacy and mathematics combined.

Case Study 10 (Technical Vocational)— TESDA

TVET for global competitiveness and work readiness

Three key challenges facing the TVET sector in the Philippines drive the strategic priorities for the next 5 years—first, the 4th Industrial Revolution (4IR) and advanced automation technologies threaten an estimated 18.2 million jobs; second, large high-growth industries will need an additional 6 million quality and skilled workers; and third, opportunities in TVET are still limited to a few, leaving out marginalized, unserved segments of the population in remote communities. These critical challenges present significant opportunities for increased investment in human capital and workforce skills development to meet the demands of 4IR. The Technical Education and Skills Development Authority (TESDA) established in 1994 is responding to these challenges given its mandate to ensure the delivery of accessible, high quality TVET.

In 2016, TESDA launched an online learning program to expand the reach of TVET. Traditional classroom-based delivery in certified TESDA testing centers limited access to those in urban locations with no means to absorb the transport cost. The high demand for TESDA programs prompted the use of technology-driven delivery to broaden reach and adopt a more inclusive approach. The TESDA Online Program (TOP) was launched as a hybrid learning model combining online and face-to-face instruction which allowed students to learn anywhere, anytime and at their own pace (Figure 33). TOP is a free, open source educational resource aligned with the changing demands of the job market and the 21st century workplace.

TESDA established industry linkages and partnered with leading private companies to ensure the quality and relevance of TVET. Co-developing programs with the private sector is essential to produce industry-relevant programs. TESDA's partnership with the private companies involved collaborative creation of courses and course content-sharing with companies such as Microsoft, Intel, Udacity-Globe, SMART Philippines, Coca-Cola Philippines, and Udemy. These are offered as part of TOP curriculum (Figure 8). Online learning materials and computer-based instructions are available in e-TESDA centers for online and offline use.

The impact of TOP as a TVET learning platform demonstrates the power and potential of technology to scale quality learning. An independent study found that nine out of ten TOP learners passed the National Assessment. TOP experienced significant growth in registered users since its launch in 2011, majority using it for skills upgrading and employment. Currently, the program has over 1.1 million registered users, of which 71.3% are enrolled learners (Figure 33). Women outnumber men, 62% and 38% respectively, with 77% of TVET learners based in the Philippines and the rest are overseas workers based in the Middle East; the United States; Canada; Singapore; and Hong Kong, China.

Case Study 11 (Higher education)— PhET Simulations

Revolutionizing Global STEM Education for All

PhET Interactive Simulations is a project originally started by Carl Wieman and his team in 2002 at the University of Colorado, Boulder, providing free, research-based, and interactive online simulations to engage students in learning science and mathematics. The project aims to promote a deeper understanding of complex concepts through interactive, game-like environments that enable students to learn through exploration and experimentation.[21]

Throughout the project (over the last 20 years), the developers focused on multiple key aspects:

- Learning Goals: PhET simulations were designed around specific learning goals derived from research-based pedagogical practices, ensuring the resources would be effective and relevant for educators and students alike.

- Research-based Design: The developers conducted ongoing research to inform their design process, incorporating user feedback, assessment data, and cognitive science research to optimize the simulations for learning.

- Accessibility and Flexibility: PhET simulations were created to be accessible to diverse learners, regardless of their background, language, or ability. Additionally, the simulations were designed to be flexible for use across various educational settings and adaptable to different pedagogical approaches.

- Playful Exploration: The PhET team aimed to create a playful environment that would encourage students to explore scientific concepts and learn through experimentation, emphasizing the value of discovery-based learning.

- Open Access: The developers made PhET simulations freely available online, ensuring widespread accessibility for educators and learners around the world.

Celebrating its 20th anniversary and as of 2022, the PhET project has delivered over 1.1 billion simulations worldwide, with more than 250 million online simulation sessions taking place on average per year. With the rise of remote learning due to COVID-19, PhET has more than doubled in usage since 2020. In Africa and Latin America, the usage growth has been even larger, increasing five times across Africa and over 10 times across Latin America. Collectively, the regions have run PhET simulations online over 64 million times since March 2020, not including any offline use.[22]

---

[21] https://phet.colorado.edu/publications/PhET_Interviews_I.pdf.

[22] Yidan Prize Foundation. https://yidanprize.org/education-initiatives/overview/phet-global-stem-education-for-all/#:~:text=Expanding%20the%20global%20impact%20of,model%20for%20impacting%20STEM%20education.

Multiple impact evaluation studies revealed that PhET's success can be attributed to its strong research-based approach, focus on learning goals, and commitment to accessibility, flexibility, and playful exploration. By engaging in iterative development processes and utilizing user feedback, the PhET team was able to create effective, engaging, and universally accessible educational resources.

In conclusion, the PhET Interactive Simulations project offers valuable insights into the successful development and propagation of educational innovations. The interviews with developers highlight the importance of research-based design, attention to learning goals, and a commitment to accessibility and flexibility. These elements have contributed to PhET's widespread adoption and effectiveness as an educational resource in science education.

Case Study 12 (Higher education)— Minerva Project: Reshaping higher education for the 21st century

Minerva is a start-up headquartered in San Francisco, California. It is a partnership between the Minerva Project and Keck Graduate Institute, a member of the Claremont University Consortium. It is reinventing college education delivery and is achieving early promise with remarkable results delivered at about one-fifth of the annual tuition cost of Ivy League schools. Its student acceptance rate (1.9% in 2016) is more stringent than that of Harvard or Stanford. Minerva's curriculum emphasizes project-based and hands-on learning. It focuses on equipping students with critical thinking, problem-solving skills, practical and vocational knowledge. After 8 months in Minerva's school, its incoming class in 2016 improved from performing in the 95th to 99th percentile on the Collegiate Learning Assessment (CLA+) compared to their peers at other colleges. Minerva also cooperates with Hong Kong University of Science and Technology to export its learning model to build a global curriculum.

In addition, Minerva has established the Transforming Learning Ecosystems (instructional curriculum design, instructor training and certification, and assessment and impact measurement), which help educators advance innovation in three key areas: the skills developed in learners, the way you teach, and how learning is measured. Taken together, these components enable improved learning outcomes for individuals at every stage, from high school, undergraduate, and graduate students to young professionals, emerging leaders, and top executives. Responding to COVID-19, Minerva launched several programs and extended their services. For example, Visiting Scholars Year is a near-term means for institutions to protect their enrollment, especially for international students or students looking to defer enrollment. The program is similar to a study abroad program, but "study remote" instead. It offers a year-long alternative to campus-based learning.

Case Study 13 (Higher education)—Udacity

Building advanced skills and industry-valued credentials through nanodegrees

As automation technologies advance rapidly, upskilling for the jobs of tomorrow becomes an imperative to secure a future-ready career. Advanced technologies require strong credentials valued and vetted by industry leaders.

Udacity developed Nanodegree programs in response to employer demand for efficient, focused, and job-relevant training for technical talent. Designed with industry experts, such as Google and AT&T, Nanodegree programs ensure students learn the exact skills needed for a particular job. Nanodegree programs are available for students of all experience levels on these areas: Programming, Data Science, Artificial Intelligence, Self-Driving Cars and Autonomous Systems, and Digital Marketing and Business. During the COVID-19 pandemic, it also offered everyone 1 free month on one of 40 premium Nanodegree programs in response to the employment disruptions and help people develop in-demand skills.

Udacity works with private and public sector partners to create scholarship programs that increase learning opportunities for merit- and need-based students across the globe. The team's goal is to ensure any interested student, including those from disadvantaged socioeconomic groups, rural areas, or unemployed youth, can benefit from a Nanodegree program.

Google Scholarships Since 2017, Udacity and Google have collaborated to offer scholarships to over 150,000 students in more than 50 countries. With a focus on web and mobile app development, the Google scholarship programs follow an innovative two-stage design that offers basic learning opportunities to thousands of students in the first phase and deep dive access through Nanodegrees to top students in the second phase. This model provides technical support and access to a vibrant student community in the initial stage, while allowing top students to benefit from tailored technical feedback and support in Nanodegree programs.

The Google India scholarship program launched in March 2018. During the first phase, 30,000 students from every part of the country learned web and Android app development. The top 1,000 students—including 300 females—received follow-up Nanodegree scholarships. Ultimately over 60% of the Nanodegree scholars finished their program and thousands of web-based and mobile apps were created by students. One student in Bangalore made an app focused on teaching Kannada, the language native to the city. A significant number of students reported strong professional growth.

Case Study 14 (Higher education and transitions to work)—JobTech.io

Powering career pathways and skills gap analysis with data science and artificial intelligence

JobTech.io is a Singapore-based company that collects and analyzes labor market data with proprietary deep AI technologies. They build products that solve static and outdated talent market problems by identifying labor market demands, recommending upskilling opportunities, performing competitive benchmarking, and automated sourcing and screening for recruitment, to create an agile and learning workforce. They shape people for careers and connect people to jobs.

Their proprietary technology stack includes:

(i)   Information extraction of skills (domain, hard and soft skills), academic qualifications, years of experience, etc. on global job postings and free text CVs.

(ii)   Recommendation engines for accurately matching upskilling and job opportunities to people directly.

The Singapore Government is working with JobTech (as well as a few other firms) to trawl the information on the internet, job boards, and talent portals to help identify new and emerging skills relevant for Singaporeans.[23] The Singapore Government publishes these insights in their yearly Skills Demand for the Future Economy report on a regular basis to inform individuals of in-demand skills and jobs to guide decisions.

Example 1: Financial tech workers are in demand in Singapore, getting multiple job offers and pay increments. Data analytics, general programming skills and knowledge of Java are the three most in-demand tech skills in the finance sector, according to JobTech's online census of job postings data this year in the sector. For example, from JobTech's data, data analytics and application engineering jobs command some of the highest median (monthly) salaries at S$7,800 and S$7,500 respectively. This type of information aids the potential job seekers in honing their skills and experience to both match the growing demand while also to gain a financially lucrative career.

Example 2: In 2021, Singapore's Ministry of Manpower announced plans to extend the SGUnited Traineeships Programme for a year, aiming to provide around 6,000 traineeship opportunities for 2022 graduates from ITE, polytechnics, and universities. JobTech has been one of the organizations supporting this initiative to enhance employability and skill development for fresh graduates amid ongoing economic challenges.[24]

---

[23]   Source: The Government of Singapore, Ministry of Education. 2022.
[24]   Channel NewsAsia (25 Aug 2021). https://www.channelnewsasia.com/singapore/jobs-graduates-traineeships-ite-polytechnic-university-2129851.

Case Study 15 (Reskill and Lifelong)— Gnowbe

The learning-on-the-go

The modern learner is time-strapped and can devote only 1% (or 24 minutes) of a typical work week for training and skills development.[25] Learning in a fast-paced work environment needs to be micro for short learner attention span, on-demand for immediate access, anytime all the time.

Gnowbe, a mobile microlearning app, was developed to meet the needs of the modern learner. Based on transformative learning theory and the science of adult learning, Gnowbe design focuses on 3 features: (1) learning-on-the-go through engaging, multimedia content sustain learner interest; (2) always-on using curated, bite-sized content for better knowledge retention; (3) on-demand for immediate anytime, anywhere access to learning content, and (4) intuitive real-time content creation. During the COVID-19 pandemic, Gnowbe provides several free or discounted COVID-19-related online courses such as infection control, business as usual in pandemic, healthcare, and so on. It also allows people to participate in Daily Pulse, a global initiative that was designed to connect people around the world through daily sessions of inspiration and interaction during the time of physical distancing.[26]

The learner's journey on Gnowbe is thoughtfully designed along a structured process of Learn–Think–Apply–Share which proceeds through a series of learning actions (Figure 39). It supports social collaboration and interactive peer-to-peer learning. Learner analytics is built in to track performance in real-time and measure learner impact. The platform is accessible as a mobile app and is also web-enabled and can be accessed using tablets or laptops. In addition, content is available through the platform from leading companies and institutions such as KPMG and Mercer if companies want to supplement third-party content with their own proprietary content. With applications used in over 20 countries, the platform has increased use in learning for those who wanted to upskill and re-skill within companies.

Course evaluation results found high student engagement (90%) and high completion rates (70+%)—about 10 times the rate of traditional e-learning platforms. In South Africa, Yes 4 Youth, a non-profit organization which promotes employment and entrepreneurship among 5 million young adults (18–35 years old), engaged Gnowbe to co-develop a course designed to improve soft skills for work, mindset and entrepreneurialism.

As a result, the program has witnessed learners spending about 305 minutes in the training modules which would indicate learners are taking great ownership of their own development. And working in collaboration with the country's local telecom

---

[25]   Bersin (2020). https://joshbersin.com/2017/03/the-disruption-of-digital-learning-ten-things-we-have-learned/.

[26]   https://learn.gnowbe.com/covid19-resources.

provider and Gnowbe's development team, the program attained zero rating for all learner-based traffic to increase usage and adoption in a country where cell phones and data are not available to everyone.

Case Study 16 (Reskill and Lifelong)— Skills Future Program

Life-long learning: Building a future-ready workforce

Singapore's SkillsFuture program is one leading example of investing in a future-ready workforce equipped with skills mastery and lifelong learning opportunities. As a national movement, Singapore's SkillsFuture has four key thrusts: (i) help individuals make well-informed choices in education, training and careers; (ii) develop an integrated high-quality system of education and training that responds to constantly evolving needs; (iii) promote employer recognition and career development based on skills and mastery; and (iv) foster a culture that supports and celebrates lifelong learning.

The program is inclusive and has targeted support for all segments of the population. For example, students can avail themselves of enhanced internships and polytechnic and technical courses to learn from meaningful work assignments and gain industry exposure to deepen application of both technical and soft skills. Through this real-world exposure, students are more informed and can make better career choices. Employees (Early Career) will have access to monetary awards to develop and deepen their skills in future growth clusters. Employees (Mid-Career) will be supported to achieve skills mastery, remain industry relevant and pursue lifelong learning as the new norm. Employers will offer recognition and rewards to all levels of staff to achieve skills mastery. Their enhanced skills become an asset as they further their contribution to the company and the industry at large. Training Providers will design and deliver quality training using technology needed to innovate and transform course delivery. Lifelong learners will have access to a wide range of resources to help throughout their learning journey.

Since its launch in 2015, more than 465,000 Singaporean adults have benefited from upskilling and reskilling from the Skills-Future Program. They also included workers in about 12,000 enterprises which benefited from the training subsidies. A major part of these training sessions were online courses—and it is one of the areas of notable success particularly for the over-25 year-old workers who needed to adapt to the skills required in the rapidly changing workplace. Courses using 25 frameworks included funding of S$500 per learner available by reimbursement to learn areas such as accountancy, aerospace, biopharmaceutical manufacturing, early childhood care, energy and chemicals, hotel and restaurant services, human resources, ICT, logistics, public transport, retail, security, tourism, and marine offshore. The workers can access online courses which are accredited from national and international suppliers of content in order to offer the variety of skills needed and futuristic skills in demand in the local market.

During the COVID-19 pandemic, Singapore launched the SGUnited Jobs and Skills Package. Building on Skills Future Programs, it aims to expand job, traineeship, and skills training opportunities to support Singaporeans affected by the economic impact of COVID-19. The SGUnited Jobs initiative will be scaled up, with a target of creating 40,000 jobs in 2020. The package will also expand traineeships through SGUnited Traineeships Programme for recent and new graduates, and SGUnited Mid-Career Pathways Programme for mid-career individuals. It is estimated to support close to 100,000 job seekers in Singapore.[27]

Case Study 17 (Reskill and Lifelong: adult learners, career switchers, and working professionals)—Udemy

Online marketplace for life-long learning and professional development

The changing nature of jobs has driven a demand for lifelong learning. By 2022, about 54% of all employees will need significant re- and upskilling, requiring additional training that may take anywhere from 3–12 months.[28] The shift in job types will be accompanied by an increasing demand for a robust set of job competencies consisting of both technical and non-cognitive, behavioral skills such as critical thinking, problem solving, leadership, communication, and collaboration. Building the capacity of future-ready workers needs to have easy and affordable access to on-demand, quality learning.

Udemy, as a global marketplace for teaching and learning, offers a wide selection of job-relevant courses. Founded in 2010, Udemy has connected learners and teachers worldwide. Its online learning platform offers video-based courses within a self-directed learning environment. Anytime/anywhere access makes learning available on-the-go using native mobile apps for iOS and Android. Today, Udemy has 50 million students in over 190 countries, 150,000 courses, 50,000 instructors, 245 million course enrollments, 30 million minutes of video, and more than 60 languages offered. Its collection of curated content covers a range of topics Development, Business, IT and Software, Office Productivity, Personal Development, Design, Marketing, Lifestyle, Photography, Health and Fitness, Music, and Teaching and Academics.

Advanced learning solutions are offered to businesses and public sector organizations. Udemy for Business serves as the corporate learning platform, which allows instant access to business-relevant content. In addition, companies can securely host and scale learning using their own proprietary training content. Udemy for Government is designed to serve the capacity building needs of public sector employees from the platform's curated content collection. Course creation tools are available for

27   https://www.ssg-wsg.gov.sg/sgunitedjobsandskills.html.
28   World Economic Forum. 2018. *The Future of Jobs Report 2023*. https://www.weforum.org/reports/the-future-of-jobs-report-2023/.

the development of job-specific skills training needs unique to the organization. Tracking employee progress and learning activities can be retrieved through the Course Insights dashboard to assess learning results and facilitate needed adjustments.

Aside from students gaining from Udemy's content, instructors who teach using the platform enjoy the advantages of a flexible schedule, reaching more students, and teaching topics they are passionate about. By teaching in Udemy, instructors earn money, inspire students, and join the community of other instructors. Teach Hub, a resource center, and Studio U, a peer-to-peer support group for instructors, aid Udemy instructors.

Case 18 (All levels)—The "Double teacher" model

Transforming Rural Education in China through EdTech and Collaborative Learning

iResearch's study shows that "individual differences in teacher's ability" and "lack of high-quality teachers" have become two biggest pain points for institutions in rural areas.[29] Two-thirds of K–12 students in the People's Republic of China are living in rural areas . A high proportion of them are "left-behind children," whose parents have gone to work in the city and do not live with their child. They are unable to receive educational support at home. However, learning resources in school are also limited there. Some K–12 schools never had English classes before since they were unable to recruit English teachers who are willing to live and teach in the area. The retention rate of teachers is high as well.

Double teacher is a blended learning model combining the online lecturing teacher and local assistant teacher to improve teaching quality and efficiency via technology especially in rural areas. It has been adopted in many education sectors in the People's Republic of China: K–12 tutoring, English language learning, and professional skill (especially IT training). According to the OECD report, teachers are spending more than 60% of their time on preparing and delivering knowledge, in which the percentage would be higher in developing countries. Teachers have limited time and energy to perform other tasks including supervising students' learning after class, mentoring students beyond academic knowledge, communicating with parents, and more. With technology, the double teacher system divided teachers' works to improve the teaching and learning efficiency.

The model works as follows: a very famous teacher, or an expert in his/her field, will be delivering the lecture online via live streaming. Through technology, this senior main teacher could livestream the session to many classrooms, in many cities, at the same time, which could extensively reduce the costs of teaching staff and solve the problem of lack of experienced teachers in a given language (e.g., English) or

---

[29]   iResearch, https://www.iresearchchina.com/.

cutting-edge technology sector (e.g., AI or VR). There will also be one assistant teacher, maybe not so senior or qualified, present in the class to make sure everyone is focused and engaged, interacting with students, answering basic questions, marking the assignment and homework, and collecting feedback. He or she could also learn different pedagogical strategies from the main teacher. This double teacher model has different variations: it can be both in a traditional offline classroom setting and online virtual classroom setting, through live streaming video (if a reliable Internet connection is available) or recorded curricula without an internet connection.

The very first company in the People's Republic of China who started to use the double teacher system is Terena, a leading professional skill education provider with a core strength in IT training in the 2000s. However, it is New Oriental and TAL Education who have pushed this concept to a larger scale.[30] They have covered over 100 remote classrooms across 20 provinces and significantly improved the percentage of college entrance exam admission rate for high school students in rural areas.

In 2018, the founder of New Oriental and TAL Education co-founded QingZinYuanShan (QZYS) foundation, which aims to provide educational support for students in rural areas via EdTech. They first launched an English double teacher program for K–12 students in rural areas. Experienced and famous teachers from Beijing are recruited as main teachers to live stream English classes and provide class materials and pedagogy. Local teachers are in charge of teaching assistance, tutoring, and student feedback. The two roles coordinate and learn with each other to establish a better learning environment for the rural students. With exposure to different pedagogical approaches, many students address the improvement of their learning efficiency and increased interest in learning English from the program. In addition to students, teachers also significantly benefit from the program. One local teacher shared that since their teacher competency and supply are limited in her school, it is difficult to launch an English program in school. However, QZYS's double teacher program not only allows students to learn and have fun, but also allows herself to constantly learn different pedagogy from the main teacher.

Since 2018, QZYS's program has experienced rapid growth. It has covered 22 provinces and served 195,000 students 6,800 teachers in the People's Republic of China. With the scaling up, the program also becomes more cost efficient. The cost per student has significantly decreased from CNY190.0431 to CNY50.63 within 1 year since the program started.

In addition to QZYS, a research team in the High School Affiliated to Renmin University of China (RDFZ) also adopted the double teacher model at the high schools with limited educational resources in remote areas. Students take classes via live streaming by the teachers from RDFZ. Local teachers are not involved in teaching but help grading, answering questions, and mentoring on the site. The results show that students in double teacher classrooms perform better than the students in the classes that have specially recruited high-quality teachers.

---

30   https://edtechchina.medium.com/two-teacher-system-the-new-model-for-the-education-training-market-in-china-63da97df0d4b.

31   CNY1 approximately equals $0.16.

Case 19 (All levels)—Learning possibility

Tools and platform supporting school data management and teaching and learning

Learning possibility provides several tools and platforms to support school data management and learning and teaching. LP+ OASIS is a web-based diagnostic tool that provides school groups or Ministry of Education (MoE) an opportunity to accurately assess their digital status and readiness through surveying all stakeholders. Stakeholders can access the questionnaire from smartphone, tablets, and PC. The assessment covers infrastructure and equipment, teaching and learning, training and skill development for digital technologies, and Learning (DTL) and Leadership and Policy. LP+ OASIS provides instant aggregation of survey results on secure cloud-based servers enabling reports to be generated immediately. LP+IDAM serves as a data management tool providing single sign-on from any devices; synchronization between on-premise and cloud. While teachers and learners move from grade to grade or switch between schools, it helps gather the data at one place, support data cleaning and standardization, allow role based multi-level access to allow local management.

Its LP+365 is a learning platform based on Office 365, which provides communication (e.g., email, Microsoft Teams, Skype, Calendar), collaboration (e.g., document share, discussions, videos), and personalization (e.g., assignments, quizzes, class notebook, language options) for teachers and learners. The platform is also fully integrated with the Teacher Support Centre, which offers teacher manuals, training videos, pedagogical ideas, etc., to enhance teacher capacity. To better integrate LP+365 into teaching and learning, LP developed the ADOPT framework, a five-stage model (Awareness, Development, Optimization, Pioneering and Transformation) defining the adoption of LP+365 to help schools to self-assess their level of development in learning platform utilization. It is selected as the national framework for the UK.

Some cost-benefit analysis studies on the LP+365 platform have been carried out.[32]

Case 20 (All levels) OpenEMIS

Education management system helping monitor and manage education systems, by offering various information management tools

OpenEMIS is an Education Management Information System that helps monitor and manage education systems, offering various information management tools, including

---

[32]   Lancaster University professor Passey"s study (2010) found that in a two-class entry school, the overall cost benefit of deploying the platform is £38,631.80. Reluctant writers and communicators engage with work on the learning platform because of the "anonymity of communication." Welsh Government Research (2016) also shows that 84% of schools strongly agree/agree that the training provided improved knowledge and awareness of appropriate usage practices; weaker students and those who dislike writing improve.

OpenEMIS Census, Core, and School, which support national education data management, individual school management, and COVID-19 vaccination tracking for staff and students.

It helps Ministries of Education monitor key performance indicators of the national plan to show progress and make mid-course corrections. It can be adopted by schools to manage administrative and teacher/student data as well. OpenEMIS includes a variety of information management systems. OpenEMIS Census facilitates the collection, processing and management of school census information. It transforms the national annual education census (questionnaires) by replacing paper forms with digital forms to rapidly collect data and generate reports. OpenEMIS Core helps the management of education information such as real-time data on individual students and staff. It is a customizable web application that supports the day-to-day activities involved in managing a sector wide education system. It builds a comprehensive national education data warehouse to track participation, inclusive infrastructure, resources, and learning assessment. OpenEMIS School is another customizable web application that supports the day-to-day activities involved in managing an individual school. It is a school information system tracking student attendance, behavior, and progress. Users can simply enter the records of the students and staff in the school to start managing day-to-day activities and generating report cards. Since COVID-19 vaccination plays an important role for schools to operate as normal and ensure students and teachers' health, OpenEMIS Vaccinations system can be used to record vaccinations by type and input health overview information for staff and students. OpenEMIS also provides other data collection, assessment, and analytical tools. These web and mobile apps work together to collect, manage, and analyze education data.

In Jordan, OpenEMIS has enabled teachers and administrators to shift away from manual registration processes, which has led to an increase in efficiency and effectiveness of national education data collection. Administrators, policymakers, and stakeholders are able to utilize the data and analysis provided by OpenEMIS to make data-driven decisions, create updated education policy, and develop programs that align the education sector with the needs of the labor market.

In Guyana, MOE is in the process of drafting 2019–2023 National Education Sector plan (ESP) and to address education sector challenges and needs. One of the challenges is that staff members are lacking the capacity to effectively collect data and monitor progress of their ESP and a lack of technological equipment. With a proposed EMIS architecture, MOE officials now aim to use OpenEMIS to collect, manage, and analyze education data. The officials have undergone the training to utilize tools to apply results-based monitoring principles to more effectively support each stage of the strategic planning cycle and monitor the implementation of all aspects of the education policy in the country.

QESA User Guide

What is the QESA EdTech Evaluation Framework and Toolkit?

Developed by the Asian Development Bank (ADB), QESA is a framework and toolkit that assists decision-makers in evaluating education technology (EdTech) products. QESA stands for Quality, Effectiveness, Scalability, and Affordability. Together, the four dimensions in QESA provide a holistic picture of the product's suitability pertaining to the organization's needs.

What is the Motivation behind the Creation of QESA?

EdTech is a crowded, confusing, and ever-evolving market. While EdTech has the potential to improve and transform education, many organizations are at a loss in evaluating and choosing a product best suited to their needs. Traditional technology assessment seldom offers a flexible approach and is not easy to keep up with the speed of technology adoption. QESA was created as an adaptable guide and a practical tool for education ministers and practitioners to use, and to help make some sense of this vast product landscape.

Disclaimer

The toolkit is intended to be a general guide that provides a balanced view in evaluating EdTech, allowing stakeholders to quickly narrow down product selections, assess the quality, gauge the feasibility of implementation, and compare similar products in the market. It is by no means definitive, as there exist other models and rubrics such as the SAMR Model, Quality Matters K12 Standards, and Comprehensive Evaluation Rubric for Assessment of Learning Apps that complement QESA.

More importantly, in selecting and implementing EdTech solutions, countries should consider their context and understand the larger environment these solutions operate. In assessing your country and ensuring institutional readiness, ADB has developed a **Digital Education Readiness Framework (DERF)**. Countries should first start with DERF before diving into EdTech product evaluation. For more information, please refer to the ADB Education Sector Group.

How to Use the QESA Toolkit to Evaluate EdTech Products?

To use the QESA Toolkit, refer to Appendix 4 (QESA EdTech Evaluation Toolkit)

The QESA Toolkit is a spreadsheet that consists of four tabs. Each tab corresponds to the dimensions in QESA: Quality, Effectiveness, Scalability, and Affordability. Ideally, you will have access to a sandbox (i.e., test environment) of the product you are evaluating whereby you can try out its features and functions, populate content, and manipulate data (dummy or otherwise). Be sure to switch around multiple user roles such as learners, teachers, admin, etc.

For the four dimensions, we define each one as follows:

- **Quality**. The extent to which the system is grounded on sound pedagogy, relevant functionality, and good user experience.
- **Effectiveness.** The extent to which the system supports the desired goals and needs of the users, is evidence-based, and has a proven impact.
- **Scalability.** The extent to which the system meets technical requirements and can scale, adapt, and evolve over time, as well as address security and privacy concerns
- **Affordability.** The extent to which the system provides value for money both for usage and for ongoing operational and sustainment costs.

Step-by-Step Guide

Step 1:	Go through each tab/dimension in the Toolkit and rank each statement using the built-in 5-point Likert Scale (i.e., Strong, Good, Fair, Weak, and Very Weak)
Step 2:	Skip over statements that are relevant to the product (i.e., Choose N/A)
Step 3:	In the Evaluator Notes column, write a brief reasoning for your scores as well as listing a few aspects that you see as strengths and weaknesses of the product.
Step 4:	Tally up the scores for each product (there is no absolute score, it is merely used as a point of comparison) and use it to position against other similar products you are evaluating.

QESA EdTech Evaluation Tool

Instructions: How to evaluate EdTech Product with the QESA Toolkit?

The QESA Toolkit is a spreadsheet consisting of four tabs. These tabs correspond to the four dimensions of QESA: Quality, Effectiveness, Scalability, and Affordability. Ideally, you will have access to a sandbox (i.e., test environment) of the product you are evaluating whereby you can try out its features and functions, populate content, and manipulate data (dummy or otherwise). Be sure to switch around multiple user roles such as learners, teachers, admin, etc.

Find QESA User Guide here.

Product QUALITY (Tab 1)		
Step 1: Audit the product	**Step 2: Use guiding questions to rate the product**	**Step 3: Reason your answers**
• Access the evaluated product to familiarize yourself with its features, functions, and content. • Make sure you try out all possible user roles: Teacher, Student, Admin, Parent, etc.	• Answer each relevant statement in the 1. Quality tab, under Functionalities, Pedagogy, UX. • Rate each statement using the 5-step scale in the drop down menu. • Leave irrelevant statements unrated (white).	• Write a brief reasoning on your score in the Evaluator Notes column. • List a few key aspects that you see as strengths of the product. • List a few key aspects that you see as weaknesses of the product. • Use the Conclusions column to sum up your findings.
Product EFFECTIVENESS (Tab 2)		
Step 1: Audit Research/Testimonials/ User Reviews, etc.	**Step 2: Use guiding questions to rate the product**	**Step 3: Reason your answers**
• Request the company to provide information related to its product's efficacy, research-basis, customer satisfaction, popularity, etc. • Audited materials can include, e.g., research articles, case studies, client testimonials, and user reviews on Appstore, and EdTech repositories.	• Answer each relevant statement in the 2. Effectiveness tab, under Evidence, User Satisfaction, and Impact. • Rate each statement using the 5-step scale in the drop down menu. • Leave irrelevant statements unrated (white).	• Write a brief reasoning on your score in the Evaluator Notes column. • List a few key aspects that you see as strengths regarding evidence on product's effectiveness. • List a few key aspects that you see as weaknesses regarding evidence of the product's effectivess. • Use the Conclusions column to sum up your findings.

continued on next page

Table *continued*

Product SCALABILITY (Tab 3)		
Step 1: Audit Product's technical specification • Request the company to provide information related to technical requirements for the use of the product. • Audited materials can include information related to device requirements, internet connection requirements, training requirements, localization possibilities, etc.	**Step 2: Use guiding questions to rate the product** • Answer each relevant statement in the 3. Scalability tab, under Infrastrcuture, Local Adaptability, and Data and Privacy. • Rate each statement using the 5-step scale in the drop down menu. • Leave irrelevant statements unrated (white).	**Step 3: Reason your answers** • Write a brief reasoning on your score in the Evaluator Notes column. • List a few key aspects that you see as strengths regarding product's scalability • List a few key aspects that you see as weaknesses regarding product's scalability. • Use the Conclusions column to sum up your findings.
Product AFFORDABILITY (Tab 4)		
Step 1: Audit Product's pricing models, payment options, costs involved • Request the company to provide information related to its product's pricing and costs. • Audited materials can include license fees, payment models, payment terms, training costs estimates, etc.	**Step 2: Use guiding questions to rate the product** • Answer each relevant statement in the 4. Affordability tab, under Investment costs, Operational costs, and Sustainability. • Rate each statement using the 5-step scale in the drop down menu. • Leave irrelevant statements unrated (white).	**Step 3: Reason your answers** • Write a brief reasoning on your score in the Evaluator Notes column. • List a few key aspects that you see as strengths regarding product's affordability. • List a few key aspects that you see as weaknesses regarding product's affordability. • Use the Conclusions column to sum up your findings.

EdTech Product Evaluation Cases Using QESA

Education Level	EdTech Product Categories	Tech Level of Application	EdTech Product Names
Preschool to Primary	Teaching and Learning	Medium	Enuma
K–12	Teaching and Learning	Low/Medium	Tangerine
K–12	Teaching and Learning	Medium/High	Akadasia
Upper Secondary to Higher Education	Teaching and Learning	Low/Medium	PhET simulations
TVET and Higher Education	Employability and Entrepreneurship	High	JobTech.io
All levels	Education Governance	Medium	OpenEMIS

Source: Authors.

(Medium-Tech, Teaching and Learning, Preschool to Primary) Enuma

The evaluation of Enuma's education technology solutions, including TODO Math, Enuma's literacy application, and KitKit School, was conducted through testing the TODO Math app, auditing available video materials, descriptions, and publicly available research papers.

Quality

Enuma's solutions offer easy access to curriculum-aligned math practices, an engaging user experience, and teacher's dashboard for progress monitoring. However, the TODO Math app lacks instructional videos and does not provide materials for fully self-directed learning. Activities do not offer guiding feedback, requiring teacher intervention for concept teaching.

Effectiveness

Enuma has conducted extensive research on product efficacy, resulting in generally positive findings, user reviews, and evidence of improved school engagement. However, more comprehensive explanations of the solutions' effectiveness and long-term impact on education quality and equality are needed.

Scalability

Enuma's solutions offer device flexibility, offline functionality, localization, and have won awards like the Global Learning XPRIZE. Pilot programs and studies have shown positive results in multiple countries. Challenges include limited access to technology, content limitations, infrastructure and training requirements, and cultural and contextual factors.

Affordability

Enuma's solutions work on more affordable devices and can be used offline, reducing internet access costs. Digital platforms can be more cost-effective at scale. A significant weakness is the lack of transparency regarding costs such as license fees, training costs, and other associated expenses on Enuma's website, which may hinder informed decision-making.

Conclusion

Overall, Enuma's education technology solutions show promise in providing accessible and engaging learning experiences, with some limitations in content and support for self-directed learning. Further research and transparency regarding costs are needed to fully assess the potential of these solutions in various contexts.

(Low/Medium-Tech, Teaching and Learning, K-12) Tangerine

The QESA assessment tool provides a framework for evaluating education technology products based on four key dimensions: Quality, Effectiveness, Scalability, and Affordability. In this matrix, we apply the QESA EdTech evaluation framework to Tangerine, a mobile assessment app designed to streamline early grade reading and mathematics assessments and enhance coaching feedback for teachers, students, and school administrators.

Quality

(i)   User Interface: Tangerine has an intuitive and easy-to-use interface that simplifies data collection, analysis, and reporting processes for educators and administrators.

(ii)   Customization: The app allows for customization of assessment content, ensuring alignment with local curriculum standards and objectives.

(iii) Data Visualization: Tangerine provides user-friendly data visualization tools, enabling users to quickly identify trends, strengths, and areas for improvement.

(iv)   Technical Support: The open-source nature of Tangerine encourages community support and contributions, ensuring continuous improvement and timely resolution of technical issues.

Effectiveness

(i) Improved Student Performance: Tangerine has been shown to have a positive impact on early grade reading and mathematics outcomes, with students demonstrating increased mastery of key skills and concepts.

(ii) Enhanced Teaching Practices: Teachers report that Tangerine's coaching feedback and data analysis tools help them refine their instructional practices and better address the needs of their students.

(iii) Informed Decision-Making: School administrators use Tangerine's data visualization tools to identify areas of improvement, allocate resources more effectively, and develop targeted interventions to support struggling students.

Scalability

(i) Platform Compatibility: Tangerine is designed to work on various mobile devices and platforms, ensuring wide accessibility across different regions and contexts.

(ii) Deployment Flexibility: The app can be easily deployed in both online and offline settings, making it suitable for use in low-resource environments and areas with limited internet connectivity.

(iii) Training and Capacity Building: Tangerine offers training materials and support resources for educators and administrators, facilitating the adoption and scaling of the app at a national level.

Affordability

(i) Open-Source Model: Tangerine's open-source nature eliminates licensing costs, making it a cost-effective solution for large-scale implementation.

(ii) Reduced Assessment Costs: By facilitating digital assessments, Tangerine helps reduce the time and resources required for paper-based tests, leading to cost savings for education systems.

(iii) Low Maintenance Costs: The app's community-driven development model ensures that updates and improvements are regularly made, minimizing the need for costly maintenance and support services.

Conclusion

Using the QESA assessment tool, Tangerine demonstrates strong performance across all four dimensions, making it a promising education technology product for improving early grade reading and mathematics assessments and enhancing coaching feedback. With its high quality, proven efficacy, scalability, and affordability, Tangerine has the potential to make a significant impact on education outcomes at the national level and beyond.

(Medium/High-Tech, Teaching and Learning, K–12 to Higher Education) Akadasia

The QESA assessment tool offers a comprehensive framework for evaluating education technology products based on four key dimensions: Quality, Effectiveness, Scalability, and Affordability. In this matrix, we apply the QESA EdTech evaluation framework to Akadasia, an online platform designed to provide accessible, high-quality educational content and resources for students, teachers, and schools.

Quality

(i)   User Interface: Akadasia features a user-friendly interface, making it easy for students, teachers, and administrators to navigate and access educational content and resources.

(ii) Content Quality: The platform offers a diverse range of high-quality learning materials, including videos, interactive modules, quizzes, and more, catering to various learning styles and needs.

(iii) Customization: Akadasia allows for the personalization of learning experiences and the ability to tailor content to align with local curriculum standards and objectives.

(iv) Technical Support: The platform provides reliable technical support to ensure smooth user experiences and prompt resolution of issues.

Effectiveness

(i)   Improved Student Performance: Akadasia has been shown to have a positive impact on student outcomes, with learners demonstrating increased understanding and mastery of key skills and concepts across various subjects.

(ii) Enhanced Teaching Practices: Teachers report that Akadasia's resources and tools help them deliver more engaging and effective lessons, better addressing the needs of their students.

(iii) Informed Decision-Making: School administrators can use data and insights from Akadasia to identify areas of improvement, allocate resources effectively, and develop targeted interventions to support struggling students.

Scalability

(i)   Platform Compatibility: Akadasia is designed to work on various devices and platforms, ensuring wide accessibility across different regions and contexts.

(ii) Deployment Flexibility: The online nature of the platform makes it easy to deploy and scale, reaching many users without the need for significant infrastructure investments.

(iii) Training and Capacity Building: Akadasia offers training materials and support resources for educators and administrators, facilitating the adoption and scaling of the platform at a national level.

Affordability

(i) Flexible Pricing Model: Akadasia provides a range of pricing options, including free access to basic content and resources, as well as affordable subscription plans for premium features and services.

(ii) Reduced Resource Costs: By offering digital educational content and resources, Akadasia helps schools and education systems save on costs associated with traditional learning materials, such as textbooks and supplementary materials.

(iii) Low Maintenance Costs: The platform's cloud-based infrastructure minimizes the need for costly maintenance and support services, making it a cost-effective solution for large-scale implementation.

Conclusion

Using the QESA assessment tool, Akadasia demonstrates strong performance across all four dimensions, making it a promising education technology platform for providing accessible, high-quality educational content and resources. With its high quality, proven efficacy, scalability, and affordability, Akadasia has the potential to make a significant impact on education outcomes at the national level and beyond.

(Low/Medium-Tech, Teaching and Learning, Upper Secondary to Higher Education) PhET Simulations

Introduction

The QESA assessment tool offers a comprehensive framework for evaluating education technology products based on four key dimensions: Quality, Effectiveness, Scalability, and Affordability. In this matrix, we apply the QESA EdTech evaluation framework to PhET Simulations, a project by the University of Colorado that provides free, interactive science and mathematics simulations for students, teachers, and schools.

Quality

(i) User Interface: PhET Simulations feature engaging, intuitive, and visually appealing interfaces that encourage exploration and active learning.

(ii) Content Quality: The simulations are research-based and designed by experts, ensuring accurate representation of scientific and mathematical concepts.

(iii) Customization: PhET Simulations offer the ability to adjust various parameters within the simulations, allowing users to tailor the experience to their specific learning objectives.

(iv) Technical Support: The project provides a range of support resources, including guides, FAQs, and a user community that shares best practices and addresses technical issues.

Effectiveness

(i)   Improved Student Performance: PhET Simulations have been shown to have a positive impact on student outcomes, with learners demonstrating a deeper understanding and mastery of key science and mathematics concepts.

(ii)   Enhanced Teaching Practices: Teachers report that PhET Simulations help them deliver more engaging and effective lessons, better addressing the needs of their students.

(iii)   Informed Decision-Making: The data and insights generated from PhET Simulations can be used by school administrators to identify areas of improvement and allocate resources effectively.

Scalability

(i)   Platform Compatibility: PhET Simulations are designed to work on various devices and platforms, ensuring wide accessibility across different regions and contexts.

(ii)   Deployment Flexibility: The web-based nature of the simulations makes them easy to deploy and scale, reaching many users without the need for significant infrastructure investments.

(iii)   Training and Capacity Building: PhET Simulations offer extensive documentation, guides, and teaching resources that facilitate the adoption and scaling of the project at a national level.

Affordability

(i)   Free Access: PhET Simulations are available free of charge, making them accessible to a wide range of users, including those in low-resource settings.

(ii)   Reduced Resource Costs: By offering digital educational content, PhET Simulations help schools and education systems save on costs associated with traditional learning materials, such as textbooks and supplementary materials.

(iii)   Low Maintenance Costs: As an open-source project, PhET Simulations benefit from continuous community-driven development and support, minimizing the need for costly maintenance and support services.

Conclusion

Using the QESA assessment tool, PhET Simulations demonstrate strong performance across all four dimensions, making them a promising education technology product for providing engaging, interactive science and mathematics learning experiences. With their high quality, proven efficacy, scalability, and affordability, PhET Simulations have the potential to make a significant impact on education outcomes at the national level and beyond.

(High-Tech, Employability and Entrepreneurship, TVET and Higher Education) JobTech

Introduction

The QESA assessment tool offers a comprehensive framework for evaluating education technology products based on four key dimensions: Quality, Effectiveness, Scalability, and Affordability. In this matrix, we apply the QESA EdTech evaluation framework to Jobtech.io, a platform that leverages artificial intelligence and machine learning to match job seekers with relevant job opportunities and provide targeted skill development resources.

Quality

(i)   User Interface: Jobtech.io features an intuitive, user-friendly interface that simplifies the job search and skill development process for job seekers.

(ii) Matching Algorithm: The platform's AI-powered algorithm accurately matches job seekers with relevant job opportunities based on their skills, experience, and preferences.

(iii) Skill Development Resources: Jobtech.io offers high-quality, personalized learning resources to help job seekers improve their skills and enhance their employability.

(iv) Technical Support: The platform provides reliable technical support to ensure smooth user experiences and prompt resolution of issues.

Effectiveness

(i)   Improved Job Matching: Jobtech.io has been shown to have a positive impact on job matching outcomes, with job seekers finding relevant opportunities more quickly and efficiently.

(ii) Enhanced Skill Development: Users report that the platform's personalized learning resources help them develop targeted skills and improve their employability.

(iii) Informed Decision-Making: Employers and workforce development organizations can use data and insights from Jobtech.io to identify skill gaps and develop targeted interventions to address them.

Scalability

(i)   Platform Compatibility: Jobtech.io is designed to work on various devices and platforms, ensuring wide accessibility across different regions and contexts.

(ii) Deployment Flexibility: The cloud-based nature of the platform makes it easy to deploy and scale, reaching a large number of users without the need for significant infrastructure investments.

(iii) Training and Capacity Building: Jobtech.io offers onboarding resources and support materials for users, facilitating the adoption and scaling of the platform.

Affordability

(i)   Flexible Pricing Model: Jobtech.io provides a range of pricing options, including free access to basic features and affordable subscription plans for premium services.

(ii)   Reduced Recruitment Costs: By streamlining the job matching process, Jobtech.io helps employers save on costs associated with traditional recruitment methods.

(iii)   Low Maintenance Costs: The platform's cloud-based infrastructure minimizes the need for costly maintenance and support services, making it a cost-effective solution for large-scale implementation.

Conclusion

Using the QESA assessment tool, Jobtech.io demonstrates strong performance across all four dimensions, making it a promising education technology product for matching job seekers with relevant job opportunities and providing targeted skill development resources. With its high quality, proven efficacy, scalability, and affordability, Jobtech.io has the potential to make a significant impact on workforce development and employment outcomes at a national level and beyond.

(Medium-tech, Education governance, All levels) OpenEMIS

Introduction

The QESA assessment tool offers a comprehensive framework for evaluating education technology products based on four key dimensions: Quality, Effectiveness, Scalability, and Affordability. In this matrix, we apply the QESA EdTech evaluation framework to OpenEMIS, an Education Management Information System designed to manage and analyze data on students, teachers, schools, and education systems.

Quality

(i)   User Interface: OpenEMIS features a user-friendly interface, making it easy for educators and administrators to input, access, and analyze data.

(ii)   Data Quality: The system promotes the collection of accurate, consistent, and reliable data, ensuring the integrity of information used for decision-making.

(iii)   Customization: OpenEMIS allows for customization to meet the specific needs of different education systems and comply with local data standards and regulations.

(iv)   Technical Support: The platform provides reliable technical support to ensure smooth user experiences and prompt resolution of issues.

Effectiveness

(i) Improved Decision-Making: OpenEMIS enables data-driven decision-making, helping educators and administrators identify areas of improvement, allocate resources effectively, and develop targeted interventions.

(ii) Enhanced Monitoring and Evaluation: The system supports ongoing monitoring and evaluation of educational programs and initiatives, promoting accountability and continuous improvement.

(iii) Data-Driven Planning: OpenEMIS facilitates the development of evidence-based plans and strategies, ensuring that resources are directed toward the most impactful interventions and initiatives.

Scalability

(i) Platform Compatibility: OpenEMIS is designed to work on various devices and platforms, ensuring wide accessibility across different regions and contexts.

(ii) Deployment Flexibility: The system can be deployed in both cloud-based and on-premises environments, accommodating the varying needs and resources of different education systems.

(iii) Training and Capacity Building: OpenEMIS offers training materials and support resources for educators and administrators, facilitating the adoption and scaling of the platform at a national level.

Affordability

(i) Open-Source Model: OpenEMIS is open-source, eliminating licensing costs and making it a cost-effective solution for large-scale implementation.

(ii) Reduced Data Management Costs: By streamlining data collection, analysis, and reporting processes, OpenEMIS helps education systems save on costs associated with manual data management.

(iii) Low Maintenance Costs: The platform's community-driven development model ensures that updates and improvements are regularly made, minimizing the need for costly maintenance and support services.

Conclusion

Using the QESA assessment tool, OpenEMIS demonstrates strong performance across all four dimensions, making it a promising education technology product for managing and analyzing data on students, teachers, schools, and education systems. With its high quality, proven efficacy, scalability, and affordability, OpenEMIS has the potential to make a significant impact on education outcomes at the national level and beyond.

References

I. Alexander et al. 2021. *Tech-Inclusive Education: A World-Class System for Every Child.* Tony Blair Institute for Global Change. https://institute.global/policy/tech-inclusive-education-world-class-system-every-child.

N. Annamalai. 2018. Exploring the Use of Facebook and Other Social Media Sites in Pre-Service Teacher Education. *The English Teacher.* 47 (1). p. 1.

Asian Development Bank (ADB), Economist Impact. 2023. *The Digital Education Readiness Framework.* https://events.development.asia/system/files/materials/2022/01/202201-digital-readiness-framework.pdf.

J.M. Beckem and M. Watkins. 2012. Bringing Life to Learning: Immersive Experiential Learning Simulations for Online and Blended Courses. *Journal of Asynchronous Learning Networks.* 16 (5). pp 61–70. https://files.eric.ed.gov/fulltext/EJ1000091.pdf.

R. Bernard et al. 2018. *Gauging the Effectiveness of Educational Technology Integration in Education: What the Best-Quality Meta-Analyses Tell Us.* DOI: 10.1007/978-3-319-17727-4_109-1.

K.L. Best and J.F. Pane. 2018. *Privacy and Interoperability Challenges Could Limit the Benefits of Education Technology.* RAND Corporation.

CEDEFOP. 2012. *European Centre for the Development of Vocational Training.* http://www.cedefop.europa.eu.

J.S. Chanduvi et al. 2022. *Where Are We on Education Recovery?* UNICEF.

J.-H. Chang and P. Huynh. 2016. ASEAN in Transformation: The Future of Jobs at Risk of Automation. *Bureau for Employers' Activities Working Paper.* No. 9. Geneva: International Labour Organization. http://www.ilo.org/actemp/publications/WCMS_579554/lang--en/index.htm.

Common Sense Media. 2022. *Common Sense Education.* https://www.commonsense.org/education/.

EdTech Impact. 2022. *EdTech Impact.* https://edtechimpact.com/.

Education Alliance Finland. 2022. *Education Alliance Finland.* Kokoa Agency Oy. https://educationalliancefinland.com/.

M. Escueta et al. 2017. *Education Technology: An Evidence-Based Review.* National Bureau of Economic Research. https://docs.edtechhub.org/lib/AEIV8XGY.

European Commission. n.d. *European Education Area: Quality Education and Training for All.* https://education.ec.europa.eu/selfie-for-teachers/how-it-works.

A. Ganimian et al. 2020. *Realizing the Promise: How Can Education Technology Improve Learning for All.* Brookings Institution.

Global Education Monitoring Report Team. 2021. *Concept Note for the 2023 Global Education Monitoring Report on Technology and Education.* Paris: UNESCO. https://unesdoc.unesco.org/ark:/48223/pf0000378950.

Government of the United Kingdom, Department of Education. 2022. *EdTech Demonstrator Schools and Colleges: About the Programme.* https://www.gov.uk/government/publications/edtech-demonstrator-schools-and-colleges-successful-applicants/about-the-programme.

H. Hansson et al. 2018. The Teachers' Portal as a Tool for Teachers' Professional Development in Bangladesh: Facilitating Nationwide Networking and Digital Multimedia Content for 40,000 Schools. *International Journal of Education and Development Using ICT.* 14 (3).

HolonIQ. 2022. Global EdTech Unicorns. *The Complete List of Global EdTech Unicorns.* https://www.holoniq.com/edtech-unicorns (accessed 8 August 2022).

A. Imchen and F. Ndem. 2020. *Addressing the Learning Crisis: An Urgent Need to Better Finance Education for the Poorest Children.* UNICEF. https://www.unicef.org/media/63896/file/Addressing-the-learning-crisis-advocacy-brief-2020.pdf.

Institute for the Study of Knowledge Management in Education. 2022. *OER Commons Platform.* https://www.oercommons.org/ (accessed 8 August 2022).

Institute of Education Sciences. 2015. What Works Clearinghouse: Using the WWC to Find ESSA Tiers of Evidence. Washington, DC. https://ies.ed.gov/ncee/wwc/essa.

International Labour Organization. 2018. *World Employment Social Outlook 2018: Greening with Jobs.* Geneva.

International Commission on Financing Global Education Opportunity. 2016. *The Learning Generation: Investing in Education for a Changing World.* New York: International Commission on Financing Global Education Opportunity.

A. Irons and S. Elkington. 2021. *Enhancing Learning through Formative Assessment and Feedback.* Routledge.

S. Isaacs. 2013. Turning on Mobile Learning in Africa and the Middle East: Illustrative Initiatives and Policy Implications. *UNESCO Working Paper Series on Mobile Learning*. Paris: United Nations Educational, Scientific and Cultural Organization.

ISTE. 2022. EdSurge Product Index. *International Society for Technology in Education*. https://index.edsurge.com/.

N. Kardaras. 2016. Screens in Schools Are a $60 Billion Hoax. *Time*. 31 August. https://time.com/4474496/screens-schools-hoax/.

E. Knight, T. Staunton, and M. Healy. 2022. About University Career Services' Interaction with EdTech. *Digital Transformation and Disruption of Higher Education*. 303.

M. Koehler and P. Mishra. 2009. What Is Technological Pedagogical Content Knowledge (TPACK)? *Contemporary Issues in Technology and Teacher Education*. 9 (1). pp. 60–70.

A. Lands and C. Pasha. 2021. Reskill to Rebuild: Coursera's Global Partnership with Government to Support Workforce Recovery at Scale. In S. Ra, S. Jagannathan, and R. Maclean, eds. *Powering a Learning Society during an Age of Disruption*. Singapore: Springer.

A. Loveless. 2002. *Literature Review in Creativity, New Technologies and Learning*. Volume 4 of NESTA Futurelab Series Report. NESTA Futurelab.

S. Lund et al. 2021. *The Future of Work after COVID-19*. McKinsey Global Institute.

M. Macià and I. García. 2016. Informal Online Communities and Networks as a Source of Teacher Professional Development: A Review. *Teaching and Teacher Education*. 55. pp. 291–307.

L. Major, G.A. Francis, and M. Tsapali. 2021. The Effectiveness of Technology-Supported Personalised Learning in Low- and Middle-Income Countries: A Meta-Analysis. *British Journal of Educational Technology*. 52 (5). pp. 1935–1964.

M. Meyer et al. 2021. How Educational Are 'Educational' Apps for Young Children? App Store Content Analysis Using the Four Pillars of Learning Framework. *Journal of Children and Media*. 15 (4). pp. 526–548. https://doi.org/10.1080/17482798.2021.1882516.

P. Mishra, M.J. Koehler, and K. Kereluik. 2009. Looking Back to the Future of Educational Technology. *TechTrends*. 53 (5). p. 49.

R. Molato-Gayares et al. 2022. How to Recover Learning Losses from COVID-19 School Closures in Asia and the Pacific. *ADB Briefs*. No. 217. Manila: Asian Development Bank. http://dx.doi.org/10.22617/BRF220301-2.

Organisation for Economic Co-operation and Development (OECD). 2015. Students, Computers and Learning: Making the Connection. *Programme for International Student Assessment Report*. Paris: OECD Publishing. https://doi.org/10.1787/9789264239555-en.

L. Pandjaitan. 2017. *IndonesiaX*. ADB Skills Forum 2016. Manila: Asian Development Bank.

R. Puentedura. 2010. *SAMR and TPCK: Intro to Advanced Practice*. http://hippasus.com/resources/sweden2010/SAMR_TPCK_IntroToAdvancedPractice.pdf.

C. Redecker. 2017. *European Framework for the Digital Competence of Educators: DigCompEdu (No. JRC107466)*. Joint Research Centre (Seville site).

REL Midwest. 2019. *ESSA Tiers of Evidence What You Need to Know*. Regional Educational Laboratory at American Institutes for Research. Washington, DC. https://ies.ed.gov/ncee/edlabs/regions/midwest/pdf/blogs/RELMW-ESSA-Tiers-Video-Handout-508.pdf.

J.M. Rosenberg and M.J. Koehler. 2015. Context and Technological Pedagogical Content Knowledge (TPACK): A Systematic Review. *Journal of Research on Technology in Education*. 47 (3). pp. 186–210.

H. Schaap. 2011. *Students' Personal Professional Theories in Vocational Education: Developing a Knowledge Base*. PhD dissertation. Utrecht University.

E.T. Straub. 2009. Understanding Technology Adoption: Theory and Future Directions for Informal Learning. *Review of Educational Research*. 79 (2). pp. 625–649.

UNESCO. 2018. Re-orienting Education Management Information Systems (EMIS) towards Inclusive and Equitable Quality Education and Lifelong Learning. UNESCO *Working Papers on Education Policy*. 5.

UNESCO. n.d. Module 3: *Improving Education Management Information Systems (EMIS)*. https://bangkok.unesco.org/sites/default/files/assets/article/Education/files/module-3.pdf.

UNESCO Institute for Statistics. 2016. ICT in Education Statistics: Shifting from Regional Reporting to Global Monitoring; Progress Made, Challenges Encountered, and the Way Forward. *UNESCO Global Education Monitoring Report*. Paris: United Nations Educational, Scientific and Cultural Organization.

UNESCO Institute for Statistics. 2022. Setting Commitments: *National SDG 4 Benchmarks to Transform Education*. Paris: United Nations Educational, Scientific and Cultural Organization. https://www.unesco.org/gem-report/en/2022-sdg4-benchmarks.

UNICEF and World Bank. 2022. *Remote Learning Packs*. Washington, DC. https://inee.org/resources/remote-learning-packs.

O. Vallo. 2022. Is Efficacy Research Killing EdTech Innovation? *EdTech Digest Column*. https://www.edtechdigest.com/2022/07/05/is-efficacy-research-killing-edtech-innovation/.

E.E. Watson and H. Schneider. 1999. Using ERP Systems in Education. *Communications of the Association for Information Systems*. 1 (1). p. 9.

A. Widiyatmoko. 2018. The Effectiveness of Simulation in Science Learning on Conceptual Understanding: A Literature Review. *Journal of International Development and Cooperation*. 24 (1). pp. 35–43.

World Bank. 2018. *Growing Smarter: Learning and Equitable Development in East Asia and Pacific*. Washington, DC. https://elibrary.worldbank.org/doi/abs/10.1596/978-1-4648-1261-3.

World Bank Group. 2016. *World Development Report 2016: Digital Dividends*. World Bank Publications. https://www.worldbank.org/en/publication/wdr2016.

World Economic Forum. 2020. *The Future of Jobs Report 2020*. Geneva. https://www3.weforum.org/docs/WEF_Future_of_Jobs_2020.pdf.

H. Yao et al. 2021. *How Much Does Universal Digital Learning Cost?* UNICEF. https://eric.ed.gov/?id=ED619426.